REVERSE AGING

Not Science Fiction,

But a Scientific Fact!

by Sang Whang

Dedication

On December 27, 1984, my father, Rev. Andrew Whang, was visiting Korea and he passed away in the studio of Far East Christian Broadcasting Company in Seoul, Korea. It was in the middle of an interview, being taped for broadcasting later on toward North Korea, when this happened. He was 78 years old then.

He did many tapings in this studio before. The topic of the conversation in this interview was longevity. The male announcer was admiring how well my father looked for his age and asked him about his secret of longevity.

My father answered: "I will tell you my secret. Well, uh,....." A few moments later, the female announcer whispered: "Oh my God!" That's how the tape ends. He had a stroke and never regained consciousness. I don't know exactly what he was planning to say.

My father, Rev. Andrew Whang, left the task of telling the world about health, longevity and reverse aging to me. Today I am pleased to dedicate this book to him and to complete the story that he began to tell the world. May he rest in peace!

December, 1990

Sang Whang

Acknowledgements

There are many people to whom I owe thanks for being able to write this book.

First of all, my wife, Mary, without whose love, help, and patience this book would never have been completed. She also made gallon after gallon of alkaline water for me and for many other neighbors for their health.

Next, my son Peter, who helped me with my computer setups and the word processing programs so that I could actually write this book. I don't know how people ever wrote a book before word processing was available. I have developed a tremendous respect for them.

Next, my daughter, Jeanne Joiner, who, in between her busy schedule with her three little children, helped me with my English so that you all can understand what I am trying to say.

Then there are many friends who believed in me and tried the alkaline water and supplied me with their positive findings. Many of them also encouraged me to write this book. Among them, I would like to recognize one special friend, Miss Therese Kim, who introduced me to the water ionizer and opened up a whole new world of health, longevity and happiness for me. Happiness is living on borrowed time.

Last, but not least, Mr. Sangik Park, who supplied me with the necessary tools and equipment so that I could carry on with the experiments. Without his generosity, patience and encouragement this book would not be here today.

Sang Y. Whang

Preface

One of the universal desires of mankind is to live long in good health. Life is the most precious gift from God.

We live in a century which has resulted in highly accelerated advancements in science and technology. At the turn of the century, man began to fly, and today we can even fly to the moon. Isn't it reasonable to expect that Science today should discover the technology of reverse aging?

Well, Science has!

The purpose of this book is to teach open minded and intelligent people to learn and practice the easy methods of reverse aging and to live long in good health. As the aging process is unnoticeably slow, so is the reverse aging process. Therefore, it is important to understand the principles and follow through the simple procedures "religiously". The process is much easier than diet and exercise, and I can assure you that you will see the effects in one year, if you follow through every day. Anything that works rapidly usually has side effects because it is not natural.

I am an engineer, scientist, and inventor with many U.S. patents. My fields of expertise span many different areas such as data communication devices (modems), electronic filters, telephone line characteristics, chemistry, water, cornea measuring devices, multi-focal soft contact lenses, etc. The secret of my successful inventions is that I don't look at problems from conventional angles. When approaching things conventionally, we come to the same dead ends that everybody else reaches.

I have looked at the problems of health and longevity, not from medical or biological scientific view points, but from the points of view of the pure science of chemistry and physics. I have studied many research works done in Japan and Germany and mentally have translated them into chemistry and physics.

Having done some consulting work for a major Japanese company, I made an interesting observation. The Japanese translate most of the research works published in English into Japanese. We, in America, translate less than 10% of Japanese research papers into English. We miss out a lot on what the Japanese are doing. It is my fortune that I speak, read and write Japanese, Korean and English.

What you will find in this book is a fresh and different approach to health and aging problems explained in simple to understand scientific terms. This book will also describe some of the conventional approaches to health and longevity problems, translated into science. You will find many interesting scientific facts about life and natural environments that you never knew before.

Introduction

In December of 1986, I was introduced to a water ionizer called "Super Ion-Q" by a friend of mine in Virginia. She told me that the alkaline water from this ionizer would lower my high blood pressure, if I drank 5 cups of it daily. In those days, I was taking 20 mg of Vasotec a day to maintain my blood pressure at around 140/90. Vasotec was my third kind of blood pressure pill. The doctor had to change my blood pressure pills twice because of different kinds of side effects. I never liked the idea of having to take any pills "for the rest of my life". That's what the doctor told me when he initially prescribed the blood pressure pills for me.

My friend didn't know exactly why the blood pressure would come down except for the fact that she knew that it worked for many people. Trusting her sincerity and knowing that she was a registered nurse, I bought the ionizer and started to drink high pH alkaline water. As I was drinking the alkaline water, I monitored my blood pressure. I reduced the amount of Vasotec gradually as the blood pressure started to come down. After 6 weeks, I stopped taking Vasotec altogether. My blood pressure came down to 130/85 without my pills.

I was elated, but at the same time I was concerned about the doubt that this could be a psychological placebo effect rather than a fact based upon some scientific phenomena. Being an engineer, I knew exactly how the ionizer produced acid water and alkaline water. The tap water had a pH value of 8.6 and the alkaline water and the acid water from the ionizer had pH values of 10.3 and 3.8, respectively. The question was, "Why did the drinking of high pH water lower the blood pressure?"

That's when I started my study. Initially the study was based upon the literature available from the manufacturer of the water ionizer. The literature was in Korean. That led me to the works done by Japanese doctors. Those works were either in Japanese or translated into Korean. The study led me to many different kinds of health improvement devices developed in Japan, and most of these devices are approved as health treatment devices by the Health and Welfare Department of the Japanese government.[16]

In the mean time, over a period of two years, I lost about 20 pounds without any special diets or exercises. I had to reduce many of my pants' waist lines about 2 inches. The clothes that I bought about 15 years ago fit me perfectly. Lately I am noticing that my eye sight is improving. I have also seen others who have gotten healthier and younger looking without diets or exercises, by simply drinking alkaline water and/or using other health treatment devices developed in Japan.

As a result of my study, I discovered the mechanics of the aging process; in other words, the hows and whys of physical aging. As I understood the process of aging, I was delighted to discover the fact that it was possible to reverse the process. When a scientist encounters a new phenomenon, he or she tries to explain the phenomenon using known theories. When these known theories cannot explain the phenomenon, a new hypothesis is created to see if that can explain the phenomenon. When many physical phenomena seem to fall into the hypothesis, the hypothesis becomes a new theory.

In this book, my theory of "Aging and Reverse Aging" is presented. This scientific theory is applied to explain, not only the process of aging, but also the developmental process of many adult diseases, such as cancer, arthritis, gout, osteoporosis, obesity, atherosclerosis, diabetes, etc. This fundamental theory can explain many phenomena that could not be previously explained.

REVERSE AGING

Not Science Fiction,
But a Scientific Fact!

Table of Contents

Dedication [2]
Acknowledgements [3]
Preface [4]
Introduction [6]

Chapter 1   The Mystery of Life and Aging [12]
             Bakster's discovery, Communications with a plant,
             Cells have intelligence, The beginning of body
             development, The beginning of aging, Immor-
             tality, Aging and reverse aging

Chapter 2   Water [17]

   2.1   General Properties of Water [17]
             Properties of water, Structure of water, Water in a
             living organism, Other properties of water
   2.2   Acid, Alkaline and pH [19]
             Acid and alkaline water, Excess oxygen in alkaline
             water, Acidity and alkalinity in our daily lives,
             Control of the sex of a baby
   2.3   Water Filters [24]
             Defense system, Defensive over-kill, Offense sys-
             tem, Water softener

Chapter 3   Food [27]

   3.1   Elements of Food [27]
             Basic elements of food; Functions of minerals,
             Calcium and Phosphorus, Potassium and Sodium,
             Iron, Magnesium, Sulfur, Chlorine; Acid food and
             alkaline food
   3.2   Waste Products of Food [33]
             Organic wastes; Inorganic byproducts; Neutraliz-
             ing functions of alkaline minerals; Acidic wastes
             that our body accumulates, Uric acid, Fatty
             acid,Phosphoric acid, Hydrochloric acid

Chapter 4   The Human Body [40]

    4.1   A Survival Machine [40]
            Acid skin prevents bacteria invasion, Influence of electric and magnetic fields, Immune theory
    4.2   Disposal System [41
            Kidneys, lungs, skin, etc.; Blood, the main carrier; Alkaline water helps the best
    4.3   Homeostasis [43]
            Blood buffers, Wastes that remain, Conversion of liquid acid to solid acid
    4.4   Life Style and Acidification [44]
            Stress and acid; Mental stress, the worst; Acidic diet and drinks; End results: storage of acids; Effects of the storage of acids; Patience

Chapter 5   Diseases [48]

    5.1   Contagious Diseases and Adult Diseases [48]
            Common causes of adult diseases
    5.2   Cancer [49]
            The Growth of cancer cells, Oxygen therapies, The True cause of cancer, Alkaline therapies, Conventional medical therapies, Best cancer prevention means
    5.3   Heart disease, Atherosclerosis, High blood pressure [53]
            Acidosis and high blood pressure, Alkaline water therapies, Pill therapies, Blood pressure and smoking, Blood pressure and sugar, Effects of soft drinks
    5.4   Diabetes [56]
            Alkaline water therapies, Adult diseases and heredity
    5.5   Arthritis, Gout [58]
            Cover-up with ointment or remove the cause, Degenerative diseases
    5.6   Kidney Disease [59]
            Kidney stones
    5.7   Chronic Diarrhea and Constipation [60]
    5.8   Other Adult Diseases [61]
            Asthma, hey fever, allergies; Hyperacidity, indigestion, gas, nausea, etc.; Osteoporosis; Morning sickness; Eye diseases
    5.9   Contagious Diseases [65]
            Edgar Cayce's prediction

Chapter 6   Reverse Aging Methods and Devices [67]

6.1   Chemical Attack [67]
              Acid forming foods, Alkaline forming foods, Balanced and mixed diet in moderation, Drinking alkaline water, Mineral supplements
6.2   Physical Attack [70]
              Exercise; Hot bath, sauna, massage, fasting, etc.; Far infrared sleeping pad
6.3   Alkaline Water Maker [72]
6.3.1   History of the Water Ionizer [72]
6.3.2   Functions of the Water Ionizer [73]
              City water and well water, Minerals in the tap water, Ionization, Increase of oxygen in alkaline water, Water pH, Commonly asked questions
6.3.3   Interesting Facts About Alkaline and Acid Water [77]
              Disinfection without boiling, Plants and acid water, Human skin and acid water, Alkaline water and cooking
6.4   The Coming Age of Far Infrared Waves [79]
6.4.1   Backgrounds [79]
6.4.2   What Are Far Infrared Waves? [79]
              Wave length of FIR, FIR penetrates deeply, Temperature and radiation frequencies, We live in a FIR temperature range, FIR wave is the safest energy source
6.4.3   How to Generate Far Infrared Waves [83]
6.4.4   Applications of Far Infrared Waves [84]
              FIR sleeping pad, FIR sauna, FIR plastic plate, Bio-Mate discs, FIR socks and gloves, FIR hair dryer, FIR vest, FIR range oven, FIR waterless egg boiler, FIR ceramic paper
6.4.5   Far Infrared Wave Clinical Treatments in Japan [86]
              Treatment for cancer, Treatment of other diseases

Chapter 7   Other Non-medicinal Health Improvement Devices [90]

7.1   Japanese Government Approved Devices [90]
              Low frequency device, Ultra short wave device, Ultra sound devices, Vibrators, Electric potential device, Infrared device, Ultra violet device, Acupressure balls, etc.
7.2   Magnetic System and Its Effect on Human Body [94]
              Magnetic sleeping system, Magnetic field prolongs mice life span

Chapter 8   Natural Environment and Health [96]

    8.1   Planet Earth [96]
    8.2   Nature's Two Kinds of Water [97]
    8.3   Electric ions in the air [98]
           Nature's air cleaning system, Effects of ions on health and mood

    8.4   Electric Potential Gradient in the Air [100]
           Potential gradient and lightning, Interaction with the ions
    8.5   Nature's magnetic field [102]
           Electric current and magnetic field, Earth's magnetic field, Magnetic field deficiency syndrome, Magnetic field and health
    8.6   Man Made Healthy Environment [104]

Chapter 9   Conventional Theories of Aging [106]

           Wear-and-tear theory; Planned obsolescence theory; Limited number of cell divisions; Glucose, the cause of aging; Cross-links, cause of many diseases; Metabolic rate theory; Free radical theory; Genes theory; Growth enzyme theory; Cryonics

Chapter 10   Conclusions and Postscript [112]

   10.1   Conclusions [112]
           Understanding the true cause of aging, Modern medical science has missed it., Simple scientific approach, Beginning of scientific research, Water, Food, Human body, The causes of adult diseases, Alkaline water is not medicine, Reverse aging methods and devices, Bright future
   10.2   Postscript [117]
           Are you a doctor?, Important facts to remember, Better than life or health insurance, Knowledge and action, We are our own nemeses, History repeats itself

Bibliography [122]

Chapter 1

The Mystery of Life and Aging

My scientific interest in the subject of "life" started in the early 70's when I did some studies on Mr. Bakster's lie detector experiments on plants.[3,19,26]

Bakster's discovery

On Feb. 2nd, 1966, Mr. Bakster, à former CIA polygraph expert, accidentally discovered that a plant can read the human mind and that this fact can be demonstrated by the use of a lie detector. I had heard of people being able to communicate with plants before, but I had never heard of being able to show it on an instrument.

Mr. Backster was watering his office plant that day and wanted to know how long it took for the water to reach a particular leaf from the time he poured the water into the pot. Since a lie detector can measure the surface conductivity of human skin, he connected the conductivity test portion of a lie detector to the particular leaf to chart the leaf conductivity variations. What he expected was a gradual increase of conductivity as the leaf received moisture from the root.

Communications with a plant

The result contradicted his expectation. The conductivity decreased; however, what surprised him more was the fact that the overall trace resembled a trace taken from a human sample. Extensive tests were conducted since that time and the results were published in the International Journal of Parapsychology, Volume X, Number 4, Winter, 1968.[3] The result is that not only do plants read the human mind, but they can also sense the emotional distress of other living things such as brine shrimp.

Since the first experiment by Backster, many scientists have conducted more tests. They have learned that we seem to communicate better with plants in the form of visual pictures rather than words. I guess that they don't understand any particular language. Also, it seems that we communicate better when we lower our brain wave frequencies to alpha waves, 8 to 16

Hertz (cycles per second), the relaxed mood. We can reach alpha waves more easily when we close our eyes and relax. Maybe that's why we close our eyes when we pray.

I was the Vice-president of research in a large electronic communications firm in South Florida in those days, and I was interested in a possible application of the mind-reading plants to detect a potential airplane hijacker. The project never took off due to a lack of funds; however, the investigation into the matter brought out realizations of many interesting facts about living cells and their local intelligences.

We all start from a single cell with a nucleus. Within the nucleus there are DNA and chromosomes which we receive from our parents. This single cell multiplies in number by splitting into 2, 4, 8, 16, 32, etc. What's interesting to note is that all these cells have the same DNA and chromosomes within one body. Identification of an individual is much more accurate by this DNA analysis than the finger print analysis.

Cells have intelligence

What's amazing is the fact that the cells with identical DNA produce different organs in a human body depending upon where they are located. In other words, the cells with identical DNA produce hair on your head while they produce finger nails on your finger. Another way to look at it is that since every cell in your body has the same DNA as the original single cell, they all have enough information to create *everything* in your body: bones, skin, teeth, eyes, heart, blood, etc.

If our skin gets cut, the cells below the surface create more skin to replace it. But when the skin grows back to the original shape, the cells somehow know to stop this growing process. This means that there is some kind of local intelligence in every cell telling them not to create anything that does not belong there, although it has the capability to create everything in one's body. This suppression of the capabilities requires many times more intelligence than what is required to create one thing.

Malignant cancer cells can be called cells that lost this intelligence. They grow things that do not belong there. This concept raises several interesting questions.

How do they lose the intelligence?

Can we restore this intelligence back to the cells?

If our mind can communicate with plant cells, can we communicate with human cells?

We don't have all the answers to these questions yet, but the first two are today within reach.

The beginning of body development

Starting from a single cell, a human body is gradually developed in an orderly manner. It is not developed in a vacuum. In order for a cell to go through the process of mitosis, duplicating itself to multiply, it requires the duplication of chromosomes. For this process, there must be a sufficient amount of proteins and amino acids in the cell to create a copy of the chromosomes. The embryo cells get these nutrients and oxygen from the womb of the mother through the umbilical chord.

The mother's blood does not circulate through the baby's body directly, but all the necessary nutrients, minerals and oxygen are transferred to the baby through the umbilical chord. The baby's own blood then circulates them throughout its body. Unfortunately, if there were any toxic substances in the mother's blood, they would also get transferred to the baby through the umbilical chord. We know all too well about babies born with drug addiction problems.

The beginning of aging

Even if there were no toxic substances in the mother's blood, the baby's body would produce waste products. The process of metabolism, the oxidation (burning) of nutrients to get energy to function, creates residue waste products that the body has to get rid of. The question is: how well, or how completely are we getting rid of all these waste products? (More about the kinds of food and nutrients and their waste products will be discussed in detail in chapter 3.)

The waste products that we do not discard completely must be stored within our body somewhere. The process of aging, which starts from the very beginning of our life, is the accumulation of these non-disposed waste products. Even when there are no toxic substances in our food, there are waste products that we must get rid of; however, if there were some harmful substances in our food, they change into poisonous wastes. The body must detoxify the poison and get rid of it.

A famous French physiologist, Alexia Carrell, kept a chicken heart alive for about twenty-eight years.[8] He incubated a chicken egg. The heart of the developing young chick was taken out and cut in pieces. These pieces, consisting of many cells, were transferred into a saline solution which contained minerals in the same proportion as chicken blood.

He changed this solution everyday, and he kept the chick's heart alive for about *twenty-eight years*. When he stopped changing this solution, the heart cells died. The secret of the chick's heart surviving for twenty-eight years lies in the fact that he kept the extracellular fluids constant and also that he disposed of the cellular waste products every day by changing the fluid in which the chick's heart was kept.

Immortality

Since ancient times, people have searched for immortality. History tells us that in almost every culture, mankind has looked for the fountain of youth or special herbs that would help them live longer. Theoretically, we are immortal. Egg and sperm combine and create new cells and new life. This new life makes egg and sperm, again forming new life. In other words, germ cells never die. A part of us lives on and on in new life indefinitely.

Eggs and sperms are germ cells. According to modern physiology, germ cells do not show signs of age, and carry the potential of life from generation to generation. (Parents may have some signs of aging; however, a baby is not born with those aging signs.) We have other kinds of cells which are ordinary body cells. As they grow, these cells turn into specialized tissue: nerve, muscle, connective tissue, tendon, cartilage, skin, bone, and fatty tissue. These tissues grow further to become specialized organs. These specialized cells of tissues and organs unfortunately reach old age and die. What makes these cells die?

Aging and reverse aging

The answer is very simple. The cells deteriorate because the waste products are being accumulated. Can you imagine a house that is allowed to throw out only 99.9% of its garbage that it produces every day? Within a few months the house will have very bad odors.

Now that we understand that the process of aging and deterioration of cells is the result of the accumulation of waste products, what we have to do is to find out the properties of these waste products and figure out a safe method of helping our body get rid of these waste products more completely, everyday. Furthermore, if we can somehow pull out old waste products that we have stored within our body from a few years ago, we will grow that much younger.

This is "reverse aging"!

I don't mean to turn the chronological clock back. I am not talking about the removal of wrinkles to look young while your interior is getting old. What I mean by reverse aging is to reduce the accumulated waste products of a 50 year old body to the level of a 40 year old body or even younger. If the accumulated waste products have not caused irreversible damage to body tissues and organs by that time, their functions could also be revived.

The following chapters of this book are designed to teach the scientific details of aging and reverse aging.

Chapter 2

Water

Water sustains all forms of life, including human life. Water is one of the most mysterious substances on this planet. Scientists are still discovering amazing facts about water. More than 70% of our body weight is water. That translates into about 10 gallons of water for a 120 lb person. You are a bundle of water wrapped in skin and walking around. Understanding water and drinking the right kind of water will give us health and longevity.

2.1) General Properties of Water

Properties of water

Water is a strong solvent; therefore, it carries many invisible ingredients: minerals, oxygen, nutrients, waste products, pollutants, etc. Inside the human body, blood (90% of which is water) circulates throughout the body distributing nutrients, and oxygen, and collecting wastes, and carbon dioxides. Every substance deep in our body was brought there by the blood and can be brought out by the blood.

Unlike any other substance, water is lighter in its solid state than in its liquid state. That's why ice floats in water. Otherwise, lakes and ponds would freeze from the bottom up in the winter time killing all living things in them. Water not only sustains life but also protects life.

Structure of water

We all know that a water molecule is H_2O, that is, two hydrogen atoms and one oxygen atom. These two hydrogen atoms are not attached to the oxygen atom in a 180^0 angle but a 104.5^0 angle in liquid state and a 109.5^0 angle in ice, making ice a more open structure than liquid water and giving it a lower density.

These angles create electric polarization effects on water molecules. The side with hydrogen is more positive than the side with oxygen. For this reason, water molecules are not disjointed, but instead they form structures that change from hexagonal to pentagonal and back, constantly, in a very short period of time (10^{-11} second) in a cooperative manner.[10]

WATER IS ALIVE!

Yes, water is alive all on its own entity without any living organism in it.

The percentage of hexagonally structured water molecules varies as a function of temperature. In pure water, there are 3 to 4% of hexagonally structured water molecules at 10^0C (50^0F) and the rest is pentagonal in structure. There are 10% at 0^0C (32^0F), and virtually 100% at -40^0C (-40^0F). We all know that a snow flake is hexagonal. The technology of the NMR (Nuclear Magnetic Resonator) is enabling scientists to see the molecular structures.

Water in a living organism

The water in a living organism is much more complex than the pure or 'bulk' water, as the scientists call it. According to Dr. Moo-Shik Chun, professor at the Korea Science and Technology Institute, Seoul, Korea, one protein molecule is surrounded by 70,000 water molecules and those water molecules form at least three different layers with different structures.[10]

Dr. Chun classifies these different layers as X, Y and Z layers. "The water molecules closely attached to the protein molecule form what is called the Z layer water and the farthest layer is the X layer which is more like the 'bulk' water. The layer in between is called the Y layer. The Z layer water is ionically bonded with the protein molecule and it is very much restricted. It is almost like solid water but will not freeze until the temperature is very low."

"The bulk water, the X layer water is quite free from the influence of the protein molecule, and it freezes at 0^0C. The Y layer water freezes at around -10^0C and the study of this layer water is important to be able to understand the health and the enzyme activities in the living organism. For example, the Y layer water surrounding an alanine dipeptide molecule has 62% hexagonal structures, 24% pentagonal structures, and 14% other structures."

18

"It can be said that hexagonally structured water is the water that living organisms like. This may explain the fact that snow-melted water is good for the growth of plankton, green algae, etc. The water from snow has high contents of hexagonal structures. Some of these results are difficult to see but are discovered and demonstrated by computer simulation methods."

Dr. Chun further explains that the Y layer water surrounding a malignant tumor doesn't have many structures. He also explains in his paper that the ionized calcium atom forms hexagonal water structures around it.

Other properties of water

Another interesting fact that scientists have discovered is that water has some degree of memory. Upon treatment by a magnetic or an electric field, properties such as surface tension and structural activities linger on for some time. Until the technology of the NMR was available, few people believed this fact. The Japanese have many magnetic and/or electric field health treatment devices. (More about these devices in chapter 7.)

Compared to other liquids, water has a high specific heat value. This fact helps our body to withstand wide variations of ambient temperature. Another important chemical characteristic of water is ionization. Ionization happens when an atom or a molecule loses its electrons or gains electrons from another atom. Even without any minerals in the water, one in ten million parts of water molecules are ionized. When a water molecule, H_2O, is ionized, the molecule splits into two parts: hydrogen ion, H^+, and hydroxyl ion, OH^-. These ions in turn ionize minerals in water to create an active chemical reaction. Since water causes ionization, without water our body ceases its chemical reactions. This means death.

2.2) Acid, Alkaline and pH

Acid and alkaline water

Sometimes there are more H^+ ions than OH^- ions in water. That kind of water is called acid water. Conversely, the water with more OH^- ions than H^+ ions is called alkaline water. When their numbers are equal, the water is called neutral water. A very interesting natural law exists in these numbers of H^+ ions and OH^- ions. When the water is neutral and the temperature is normal room temperature, the ratio of H^+ ions to the total water molecule is $1:10^7$. If we call the total number of water molecules to be 1 unit, the total number of H^+ ions in this neutral water is 1×10^{-7} unit. Since the neutral water has an equal number of OH^- ions, it is also 1×10^{-7} unit. In short, we say that the pH of this water is 7.

If acid minerals such as sulphur or chlorine are added to this water, the number of H^+ ions increases because the hydrogen atoms give away electrons to the acid minerals. When the number of H^+ ions increases to 1×10^{-6} unit (ten times that of neutral water), the law of nature forces the number of OH^- ions to decrease to 1×10^{-8} unit. The pH of this water is 6. The sum of the exponents for H^+ ions and OH^- ions always adds up to 14 in room temperature water ($22^{\circ}C$). There is no need to say that the pOH of this water is 8. It is understood. For this reason, we only measure the concentration factor of the hydrogen ion and not the hydroxyl ion.

Examples of some pH values of water and the concentrations of H^+ ions and OH^- ions are given below.

pH	pOH	H^+ concentration	OH^- concentration
2.5	11.5	$1\times10^{-2.5} = 3.163\times10^{-3}$	$1\times10^{-11.5} = 3.162\times10^{-12}$
4.0	10.0	$1\times10^{-4.0} = 1.000\times10^{-4}$	$1\times10^{-10.0} = 1.000\times10^{-10}$
6.0	8.0	$1\times10^{-6.0} = 1.000\times10^{-6}$	$1\times10^{-8.0} = 1.000\times10^{-8}$
7.0	7.0	$1\times10^{-7.0} = 1.000\times10^{-7}$	$1\times10^{-7.0} = 1.000\times10^{-7}$
7.3	6.7	$1\times10^{-7.3} = 5.012\times10^{-8}$	$1\times10^{-6.7} = 1.995\times10^{-7}$
7.45	6.55	$1\times10^{-7.45} = 3.548\times10^{-8}$	$1\times10^{-6.55} = 2.818\times10^{-7}$
8.0	6.0	$1\times10^{-8.0} = 1.000\times10^{-8}$	$1\times10^{-6.0} = 1.000\times10^{-6}$
9.0	5.0	$1\times10^{-9.0} = 1.000\times10^{-9}$	$1\times10^{-5.0} = 1.000\times10^{-5}$
9.5	4.5	$1\times10^{-9.5} = 3.162\times10^{-10}$	$1\times10^{-4.5} = 3.162\times10^{-5}$
10.0	4.0	$1\times10^{-10.0} = 1.000\times10^{-10}$	$1\times10^{-4.0} = 1.000\times10^{-4}$

We think that water is H_2O, that is, two hydrogen atoms for each oxygen atom. However, this exact 2 to 1 ratio exists only in a water with a pH of 7, where the number of H^+ ions is the same as the number of OH^- ions. Since alkaline water has less H^+ ions than OH^- ions, this water has more oxygen atoms than half of the hydrogen atoms. Conversely, acid water has more H^+ ions than

OH⁻ ions; therefore, this water has less oxygen atoms than half of the hydrogen atoms.

Human blood has a pH value ranging from 7.3 to 7.45. From the table above, the excess OH⁻ ions in the water with a pH value of 7.45 is 2.463×10^{-7} ($2.818 \times 10^{-7} - 0.3548 \times 10^{-7} = 2.4632 \times 10^{-7}$). The excess OH⁻ ions in the water with a pH value of 7.3 is 1.494×10^{-7}. Blood with a pH value of 7.45 contains 64.9% more excess oxygen than blood with a pH value of 7.3. The pH values of 7.3 and 7.45 seem almost the same, but there is a big difference in the amount of excess oxygen between the two examples of blood.

Excess oxygen in alkaline water

Ten ounces of water weighs approximately 0.296 kilogram. Since the atomic mass unit of a water molecule is 18 and one atomic mass unit is 1.66×10^{-27}kg, one water molecule weighs 29.88×10^{-27}kg.[13] This means that there are approximately 1×10^{25} number of water molecules in 10 oz. of water.

Knowing the pH values of different drinks, one can calculate the number of H⁺ ions and OH⁻ ions in a particular glass of water. The following table compares the pH values and the excess oxygen counts (or oxygen deficiency counts in some cases) in different 10 oz. drinks.

	pH	H⁺	OH⁻	exc. oxygen
Popular brand cola	2.5	3.162×10^{22}	3.162×10^{13}	-158.1×10^{20}
Diet soft drink	3.2	6.310×10^{21}	1.585×10^{14}	-31.55×10^{20}
Popular brand beer	4.7	1.995×10^{20}	5.012×10^{15}	-0.998×10^{20}
R.O. filtered water	6.8	1.585×10^{18}	6.310×10^{17}	-0.005×10^{20}
Distilled water	7.0	1.000×10^{18}	1.000×10^{18}	0.000
Typical bottled water	7.8	1.585×10^{17}	6.310×10^{18}	0.031×10^{20}
Filtered tap water*	8.4	3.981×10^{16}	2.512×10^{19}	0.125×10^{20}
Alkaline water**	10.0	1.000×10^{15}	1.000×10^{21}	5.000×10^{20}

   * Typical Miami tap water
   ** Alkaline water made from typical Miami tap water

The effects of drinking different pH liquids for a human body will be discussed later; however, I would like to make one observation from the table above. All kinds of soft drinks are very acidic, especially colas. In order to neutralize a glass of cola, it takes about 32 glasses of high pH alkaline water.

A glass of cola (with a pH value of 2.5) added to 10 gallons of water with a pH value of 7.4 will lower the pH of 10 gallons of water to 4.6. A human body contains about 10 gallons of slightly alkaline water. Fortunately, drinking a glass of cola does not lower the pH value to 4.6. It would be fatal. The capability of homeostasis and how the blood maintains a pH of 7.3 to 7.4 when we drink highly acidic cola will be discussed later in detail.

Acidity and alkalinity in our daily lives

Acidity or alkalinity is all around us, even aside from the drinks. For example, baking soda has a pH value of 12.0; soap, 9.1; sea water, 8.1; lemons, 2.3; apples, 3.1; bananas, 4.6; potatoes, 5.8; oysters, 6.4; shrimp, 6.9; salt, 7.5; etc. ("Acid & Alkaline" by Herman Aihara[1]) The fact that a certain food measures with an acidic pH does not necessarily mean that the food influences our body to become more acidic. (More about acid tasting and acid forming foods will be discussed in Chapter 3.)

We measure the pH of a liquid solution with a pH meter or with blue and red litmus papers. Today there is a special liquid tester that changes colors depending upon the pH changes. For example:

pH	color
4	orange
5	yellow
6	light green
7	green
8	blue
9	dark blue
10	purple

If we had a special pair of glasses that would show all of these colors depending upon the pH values as shown above, the world would be a colorfully different place. You might ask, what is the practical use for that? One very useful application may be that if I could look at person's skin with such glasses, I might detect some spot with uneven coloration which may enable me to diagnose the physical problem that particular person has. Human skin is acidic while the blood and the cells are slightly alkaline. Healthy skin will display an even orange-yellow color through these glasses.

Speaking of human body pH, the following table shows the average pH values of some human body liquids.

	pH
Stomach juice	1.5
Skin	4.7
Saliva	7.1
Cell	7.1
Blood	7.4
Pancreatic juice	8.8

Control of the sex of a baby

With an understanding of human body fluid acidity and alkalinity, one can control the sex of a baby before it is conceived. Male sperm is alkaline while the inside of the vagina is acidic. The sperm with a male chromosome swims rapidly but lives only for a short time in an acidic environment. The sperm with a female chromosome swims slowly but lives longer in an acidic environment.

Knowing these simple facts you can increase the chances of making either a boy or a girl, which ever you want. If the egg is there first waiting for the sperm to arrive, the chances are that the male chromosome sperm will get to the egg first. However, if the sperm is there first, waiting for the egg to come out, chances are that the female chromosome sperm will be the surviving ones.

If the parents drink alkaline water for over a month prior to conception, the sperm and the inside of the vagina will become more alkaline and they have increased the odds of making a boy significantly. I don't know how accurate it is, but a document from Korea says that the odds of making a boy are 95% if both partners have been drinking alkaline water for at least 30 days prior to conception.

In Korea there is a shortage of baby girls right now, and this is creating a social problem.

2.3) Water filters

When we talk about the subject of "water and health", we usually think of water filters. It's a known fact that the quality of water in this country is getting worse. Health conscious people are drinking bottled water or have some kind of a water filter in their kitchen. Bottled water is usually filtered tap water. The main purpose of any water filter is to remove harmful pollutants in the water so that they won't enter our body. It's a defensive device.

Defense system

City supplied tap water comes in many different qualities. In order to kill bacteria and microbes, they put chlorine in the water. Chlorine is a good disinfectant, but it is harmful if ingested in large quantities. Not only that, it combines with hydrocarbons in the water to form carcinogenic chlorinated hydrocarbons. This is the most common pollution problem throughout our country.

The most cost-effective filters for chlorine and chlorinated organic substances are charcoal filters. Compressed carbon block filters or activated granular charcoal filters are the types that are commonly available. Among the two, the better choice is the compressed carbon block filters for several technical reasons.

Activated granular charcoal filters rely on the surface adsorption of chlorine and chlorinated hydrocarbons, but as such there is no mechanical constriction of any solid particles in the water. And when the carbon is all used up, it continues to supply unfiltered water. It requires the customer to check for the chlorine to see if the filter is still working. Usually this type of filter comes with silver impregnation to prevent bacterial growth inside the filter.

Compressed carbon block filters not only eliminate chlorine and chlorinated hydrocarbons by its carbon, but they also mechanically constrain the flow of water to trap heavy metal particles and bacteria. Usually this type of filter does not require silver impregnation. The only drawback is that the water pressure drops considerably as one use the filter. Usually the water flow gets intolerably slow before the carbon loses its potency. This means that as long as the water is coming out, the water is good. When the water flow is too sluggish, replace the cartridge.

If the compressed carbon filter is used in conjunction with some other device, such as a water ionizer to make alkaline water, the pressure drop becomes a problem. For such an application, the activated granular charcoal filters mentioned above are recommended.

Defensive over-kill

A person can wear steel armor that is so heavy that he is unable to move at all and could thusly be caught by the enemy. This is called defensive over-kill. One can go overboard on water filters too.

In an attempt to get "pure" water, some people promote distillers and reverse osmosis (R.O.) filters. While these devices work well, they take *everything* out of the water. Unfortunately, this "pure" water is not healthy. It's dead water. Fish cannot live in it. If ingested for long periods of time, it can leach out valuable body minerals, such as potassium, magnesium, sodium and calcium. One can take mineral supplements to replace them; however, it's not easy to replace the minerals in our body in the same form that we lost them in.

Those who market distillers or R.O. filters insist that the less substance remaining in the water, the better the water is. They use a TDS tester to measure the amount of total dissolved solids in the water, whether they are good or bad. Water rich with good minerals will test as very bad water with this TDS tester. Unfortunately, both the sellers and the buyers of these distillers and R.O. filters believe that water without anything in it is the best. As shown in section 2.2 above, this water contains no extra oxygen. If the distilled water or the R.O. filtered water is used with a water ionizer, nothing happens. No alkaline water or acid water will be produced.

Offense system

Now let us focus our attention on the offense in order to win in the game of health and water. As mentioned in chapter 1, the process of aging is the accumulation of old waste products within our body. In the next chapter, we will discuss the kind of waste products that food generates within the body. *These waste products are acidic.*

The goal of the game is to help your body dispose of more acidic waste products. The more the better. Since waste products are carried out by the blood and disposed of in liquid form, drinking the right kind of water can score more points. The best kind of water for this function is acid-free alkaline water, the water that neutralizes harmful acids and disposes of them safely while it does not leach out valuable alkaline minerals such as potassium, magnesium, sodium, calcium.

The device necessary to make the acid-free alkaline water is called a water ionizer. The principle of this water ionizer is fully explained in chapter 6 and the scientific reasons why and how this alkaline water scores points in reverse aging and prevention of many adult diseases are discussed in chapter 5.

There is no other water treatment device that produces oxygen rich alkaline water with the pH of 10. You can spend a fortune to take out some imaginary harmful chemical substances that are not even in your water. Watch out for scare tactic sales promotions.

Water softener

In a related product, there is a water softener. The hardness of the water is determined by the calcium contents. A water softener replaces calcium ions with sodium ions. The sodium comes with chlorine and the resultant water becomes more acidic. The water is great for house pipe systems and you *do* save in detergent on your washing machine. *But the water is not healthy to drink.* Reputable water softener companies provide a separate water path to the kitchen for drinking water for this reason.

Chapter 3

Food

Some eat to live while others live to eat. Some foods taste great while some are unpalatable. Some foods are expensive while others are not. They say that some foods are good for your health while some others can damage your health. There are so many books written about cooking, diet, health food, etc. It is one of the most confusing issues of the past few decades.

At the risk of taking all the romance away from the art of eating and gourmet cooking, I am going to look into the basic elements of our foods and the waste products produced from these foods after they are metabolized in our cells.

3.1) Elements of Food

Basic elements of food

In order for our body to function and grow, we must eat food. Food is generally classified into three categories: carbohydrates, proteins and fat. All of these foods are made of four basic elements: carbon, nitrogen, oxygen and hydrogen. Carbohydrates do not contain nitrogen. All four elements are abundant in the air; therefore. manna from heaven is not too difficult to understand. Now that Science has discovered the process of reverse aging, the next challenging frontier for scientists should be the development of food from the air to solve the world's hunger problems.

Mixed in with these foods with four elements are many inorganic minerals such as sulfur, chlorine, sodium, calcium, etc. They are classified into two categories, namely acid forming elements and alkaline forming elements.

Acid forming elements	Alkaline forming elements
sulfur (S)	sodium (Na)
phosphorus (P)	potassium (K)
chlorine (Cl)	calcium (Ca)
iodine (I)	magnesium (Mg)
	iron (Fe)

According to Dr. Arthur Guyton[14], The average amount of minerals in a 154-lb. adult male is:

Acid forming elements		Alkaline forming elements	
Cl	85.000 gr.	Na	63 gr.
P	670.000 gr.	K	150 gr.
S	112.000 gr.	Ca	1,160 gr.
I	0.014 gr.	Mg	21 gr.
		Fe	3 gr.

Functions of minerals

These minerals exist throughout the human body, and according to 'The Yearbook of Agriculture'[27], 'Medical Physiology' by Arthur Guyton[14], 'Encyclopedia of Biochemistry', and 'Acid & Alkaline' by Herman Aihara[1], these minerals totaling about 5 lbs provide essential functions to sustain our body. The following contain some excerpts from these references describing functions of these minerals and foods that contain these minerals.

Calcium and Phosphorus (Ca and P)

About 99 percent of the calcium and 80 to 90 percent of the phosphorus in our body are in the bones and teeth. The rest can be found in the soft tissues and body fluids and are highly important to their normal functioning. Calcium in a complex combination with phosphorus gives rigidity and hardness to the bones and teeth. Irritability of the nerves is increased when the amount of calcium in the blood is below normal.

When there is no reserve to use, the calcium has to be taken from the bone structure itself, usually first from the spine and pelvic bones. From 10 to 40 percent of the normal amount of calcium may be withdrawn from mature bones before the deficiency will show up on X-ray.

The calcium that is absorbed travels in the blood to places where it is needed, particularly to the bones. If any of the absorbed calcium is not needed, it is excreted by the kidneys into the urine. Normal functioning of the kidneys is essential for the normal metabolism of calcium and other minerals.

Phosphorus is an essential part of every living cell. It takes part in the chemical reactions with proteins, fats and carbohydrates to give the body energy and vital materials for growth and repair; for example, phospholipids are important in the synthesis of cell membranes and synthesis of DNA and RNA.

Some of the foods that contain calcium minerals are seaweed, black sesame seeds, tofu, milk, yogurt, carrot leaves, green scallions, spinach, etc. The foods that are rich in phosphorus mineral are miso, eggs, salmon, mackerel, tuna, bonito, codfish, chicken, black sesame seeds, seaweed, white rice, pork, etc. (Herman Aihara's "Acid & Alkaline"[1] gives a rather extensive list of different foods and their mineral contents. For this type of information, I refer you to the macrobiotic reference books in your health food stores.)

Potassium and Sodium (K and Na)

Sodium and potassium are similar in chemical properties but different in their location within the body. Sodium is chiefly in the fluids that circulate outside the cells, and only a small amount of it is inside the cells. Potassium is mostly inside the cells, and a much smaller amount is in the body fluids

Sodium and potassium are vital in keeping a normal balance of water between the cells and the extra cellular body fluids. A decline in the sodium content of the body fluids results in a transfer of water from the fluids to the cells. An increase in sodium causes a transfer of water from the cells to the fluids.

Sodium and potassium are essential for nerves to respond to stimulation, for the nerve impulses to travel to the muscles, and for the muscles to contract. All types of muscles, including the heart muscle, are influenced by sodium and potassium. It is important to maintain the proper ratio of these two minerals.

Sodium and potassium also work with proteins, phosphates, and carbonates to keep a proper balance between the amount of acid and alkali in the blood. Sodium and potassium are taken in in the form of salt. A large amount of potassium is found in soybeans, carrots, potatoes, and fruits such as apricots, avocadoes, bananas, dates, oranges, and watermelon. Salty meat such as bacon, ham, and corned beef contain high amounts of sodium, while white meat such as chicken, duck, lamb, and pork contain more potassium than sodium.

Iron (Fe)

The major proportion of iron in the body is in the form of hemoglobin, though smaller quantities are present in other forms, especially in the liver and in the bone marrow. Electron carriers containing iron are present in all the cells of the body and are essential for most of the oxidation that occurs in the cells. Therefore, iron is absolutely essential both for the transport of oxygen to the tissues, and for the maintenance of oxidative systems within the tissue cells, without which life would cease within a matter of seconds.

Vegetables are a good source of iron, and so is miso soup. Meat, chicken, and fish have traces of iron, and cow's milk and human milk also have small amounts of iron. However, the best sources of iron are animal liver and canned prune juice.

Magnesium (Mg)

Magnesium is closely related to both calcium and phosphorus in its location and function in the body. About 70% of the magnesium in the body is found in the bones. The rest is in the soft tissues and blood. Muscle tissue contains more magnesium than calcium. Blood contains more calcium than magnesium.

According to Arthur Guyton, "An increased extracellular concentration of magnesium depresses activity in the nervous system and also depresses skeletal muscle contraction. This latter effect can be blocked by administration of calcium. Low magnesium concentration causes greatly increased irritability of the nervous system, and cardiac arrhythmias."[14]

Magnesium is found in general with calcium. Meat contains magnesium, and so do many fruits.

(Of the five alkaline minerals, potassium has the strongest chemical reaction power, followed by sodium, calcium, magnesium, and finally iron. This means that calcium can kick out magnesium from a magnesium-salt but not the other way around.)

Sulfur (S)

Sulfur is found in its elementary state mixed with earthy matter in volcanic districts, the chief supply being derived from Sicily. Sulfur in some form is required by all living organisms. It is utilized in various oxidation states including sulfide, elemental sulfur, sulfite, sulfate and thiosulfate by lower forms, and in organic combination by all. The more important sulfur-containing organic compounds include: the amino acids, cysteine, cystine,and methionine which are components of protein.

"In the organic world sulfur is built in the protein molecules of the plant from the sulfates taken from the soil. It is chiefly taken up by the animal organism in the form of protein, and secreted for the most part in the highest oxidized condition as sulfuric acid, derived from the splitting up and oxidation of the protein molecule. In this form, combined and neutralized by alkalies, it is again ready to begin the cycle of life, by forming organic sulfur compounds in plants." (Carque, "Vital Facts About Foods"[7])

Egg is a good source of sulfur, and so are many vegetables.

Chlorine (Cl)

Chlorine is found chiefly in sodium chloride or common salt, either dissolved in water or as a solid deposit in the interior of the earth in the form of rock salt. It is poisonous as a gas.

Chlorine, in the form of sodium chloride, plays an important part in the animal organism. It assists in the formation of all the digestive juices, principally of the gastric juice, which contains two parts per 1 mille hydrochloric acid. The mineral matter of the blood serum is made up largely of sodium chloride, which favors and sustains the generation and conduction of electric currents. Chlorides are useful, not only in the construction of the organs but also in the preparation of the digestive secretions.

Chlorides are likewise important for anal secretion. They are necessary for the elimination of the nitrogenous waste products of metabolism.

Reviewing many references on foods and their contents, I noticed an interesting fact. On the average, 70 to 90% of food by weight is water, except for dried foods. The amount of inorganic minerals in non-processed food is less than 1% in general and about 0.5% on the average. Processed food, bacon for example, contains minerals as much as 7% of its weight. As you can guess, most of the minerals are in the form of sodium chloride.

Excluding water, more than 97% of our food consists of carbohydrates, proteins, fiber and fat, which are made out of four elements: carbon, nitrogen, hydrogen and oxygen. Less than 3% of our food is inorganic minerals.

Acid food and alkaline food

These inorganic minerals in the food determine whether the food is alkaline or acidic. When dieticians talk about acidic food or alkaline food, they are not talking about how they taste. For example, orange juice tastes acidic (a pH of 3.5), but this acidity is generated by organic acids which can all be burnt away. However, inside the orange, there are alkaline minerals such as potassium and magnesium; therefore oranges are considered to be an alkaline forming food. The dieticians are concerned about the residual effects of the food after digestion and metabolism in our cells. The following is an excerpt from "Acid & Alkaline"[1]

"How to Determine Acid Forming Foods
    and Alkaline Forming Foods"

"In theory, whether a given food is acid forming or alkaline forming is determined by the proportion of acid forming and alkaline forming elements contained in the food. In practical reality, however, it is determined by test tube. This procedure is known as titration.

First, the food to be measured is burned to ashes. (It is this step of burning the food that takes the place of digestion and thus gives us a picture of whether the food is acid or alkaline forming.) Next, a standard amount of very pure water, say one liter, is added to 100 grams of these ashes to make a solution. This solution is tested to see whether is acid or alkaline. Once we know whether the solution is acid or alkaline, we can measure the concentration or strength of the acidity or alkalinity of the ash solution.

Since an acid solution will neutralize or cancel an alkaline solution, and vice versa, the two can be used to measure each other."

From the previous chapter, you can figure out the numbers of H^+ ions and OH^- ions in any volume of water with a known pH value. Therefore, knowing the number of ions that it took to neutralize the given volume of food ash solution, it is easy to figure out the strength of the acidity or alkalinity.

According to this kind of test, foods are classified and tabulated in the order of the concentration of acidity and alkalinity. Many macrobiotic diet books, including the one by Herman Aihara, contain tables with acid forming foods and alkaline forming foods.

The big assumption made in this type of determination is that the food will be completely oxidized (metabolized) by the cells; therefore, the acidity or alkalinity of the food residue (ash) is exclusively determined by these inorganic minerals. Unfortunately, 97% of all foods (C, N, H and O) do not burn completely and they leave organic acidic waste products, with no help from the inorganic acid minerals. Uric acid and lactic acid are some of the examples of organic acid wastes created by our body.

3.2) Waste Products of Food

Organic wastes

The amount of these organic acid wastes created is much greater than the acidic or alkaline residues created by the inorganic minerals in food. For this reason, even if you eat nothing but alkaline forming foods, your urine will be acidic and so will your perspiration. Chemical formulas of some of the better known organic waste products that our body produce are shown below.

Acetic acid	CH_3COOH	Ammonia	NH_3
Lactic acid	$CH_3CHOHCOOH$	Uric acid	$C_5H_4N_4O_3$
Cholesterol	$C_{27}H_{45}OH$	Fatty acid	$C_nH_{2n}O_2$
Carbonic acid	H_2CO_3		

Among these wastes, ammonia comes out through the urine, and carbonic acid can become water by breathing out CO_2 through the lungs.

Inorganic byproducts

Besides these organic wastes, there are many inorganic mineral byproducts from the minerals found in food. The poisonous acidic products derived from sulfur, phosphorus and chlorine in our food are:

Sulfuric acid $\quad\quad$ H_2SO_4 $\quad\quad$ Phosphoric acid $\quad$ H_3PO_4
Hydrochloric acid $\quad$ HCl

These poisonous acids must be disposed from our body. But before that they must be neutralized to become less harmful substances. Otherwise, they can damage the kidneys and other organs. Products neutralizing these poisons are also produced by our body from alkaline minerals found in food. These alkaline minerals are sodium, potassium, calcium and magnesium. The neutralizing products are:

Sodium carbonate $\quad\quad$ Na_2CO_3 $\quad\quad$ Sodium bicarbonate $\quad$ $NaHCO_3$
Potassium carbonate $\quad$ K_2CO_3 $\quad\quad$ Calcium carbonate $\quad\quad$ $CaCO_3$
Magnesium carbonate $\quad$ $MgCO_3$

Neutralizing functions of alkaline minerals

As an example, sulfuric acid can be neutralized by calcium carbonate as follows.

$$CaCO_3 + H_2SO_4 = CaSO_4 + H_2O + CO_2$$

Poisonous sulfuric acid is changed into neutral calcium sulfuric salt, water and carbon dioxide. H_2O and CO_2 form the familiar carbonic acid (H_2CO_3), which is volatile. In the equation above Ca can be replaced by Mg, Na_2, or K_2. As long as there are sufficient amounts of alkaline minerals in the body, poisonous acids are neutralized. When there is not an adequate supply of calcium or other alkaline minerals in the blood, sometimes the body borrows calcium from bones to survive.

Another acid neutralizing compound is ammonia NH_3, which our body produces from protein food. Hydrochloric acid, HCl, becomes NH_4Cl, ammonium chloride. Sulfuric acid, H_2SO_4, becomes ammonium sulfate, $(NH_4)_2SO_4$.

Acidic wastes that our body accumulates

Let's examine some of the organic and inorganic acids that we have a tendency to keep within our body. After all, most of these are produced by 97% of our foods.

Uric acid:

Webster says, "Uric acid is a white, odorless crystalline substance found in urine, being one of the products of nuclein metabolism. It is nearly insoluble in water, alcohol, and ether, but soluble in solutions of alkaline salts."

These undissolved uric acid crystals can accumulate between joints and can cause arthritis and gout. It doesn't happen when you are young because your body is more alkaline and the uric acid gets dissolved and safely discharged through the kidneys.

Fatty acid:

Over-ingestion of carbohydrates and not enough exercise (not enough burning away) causes our body to store fatty acids. Acetic acid, lactic acid and cholesterol are the derivatives of fatty acid. When athletes over-exercise, there is not enough oxygen in the cells and this creates lactic acid and acetic acid, which are incompletely burnt carbohydrates.

Lactic acid and acetic acids lower the pH of body fluids drastically. In order to survive, they tax body alkaline minerals to elevate the pH value. If we abbreviate lactic acid as HL, the process of neutralization can be shown as below.

$$HL + NaHCO_3 = NaL + H_2O + CO_2$$

(If we replace L with Cl in the above equation, the equation will show the process of neutralizing hydrochloric acid, HCl.)

A fatty acid molecule is a long chain of carbon and hydrogen atoms and so is a cholesterol molecule. When blood contains too much of these fatty acids, lactic acid and acetic acid, it tends to drag down the blood pH. Many complicated actions take place to maintain the blood pH within the safe range. A buffer system in the blood, in the form of alkaline salts, works hard to neutralize the acids. Another solution is to solidify some of the liquid acids into solid acids, in a non dissolved acid form.

Cholesterol is one of those examples. For this reason, even if you don't eat any food containing cholesterol, your body makes cholesterol, as long as you are eating and generating acidic byproducts. Uric acid becomes solid urate and phosphoric acid becomes solid phosphate, etc. (See next section.)

We are all familiar with the role that cholesterol plays with blood circulation problems, heart ailments and plaque build-up in the arteries. One thing that we are not too familiar with is the fact that acid coagulates blood. Mouth wash and after shave lotions are acidic thus they stop bleeding. Having the tendency to coagulate blood and the molecules having long chains of carbon and hydrogen atoms (like hydro-carbons), cholesterol is very conducive to generating blood clots also.

Phosphoric acid:

Most proteins in food combine with sulfur and phosphorus. When the protein is metabolized, these elements remain as sulfuric and phosphoric acid and must be neutralized by ammonia and alkaline minerals before they can be discharged safely by the kidneys. Most grains also contain much sulfur and phosphorus, creating sulfuric and phosphoric acid.

A kidney stone is a hard mineral deposit formed in the kidney from phosphates (a salt of phosphoric acid), urates (a salt of uric acid), etc., according to Webster. A salt of phosphoric acid contains some amount of calcium used to neutralize the highly poisonous phosphoric acid. For this reason, a kidney stone looks like a white calcium deposit.

Some people mistakenly blame excess calcium as the cause of kidney stones. The best way to differentiate calcium deposits from kidney stones is the urine test. Calcium deposits dissolve in urine while kidney stones do not. Kidney stones dissolve in an alkaline solution.

As we age, we build up these acid salts in our cells as well, causing our cells to stiffen (even without the glucose bonding of protein molecules). Some dieticians claim that the cause of aging is the accumulation of calcium in our cells and they promote magnesium supplements to unlock calcium deposits in the cell. Magnesium is weaker than calcium and it cannot kick out calcium from a calcium salt. The reason why magnesium seems to work is that it makes the environment more alkaline so that the acid salts such as phosphates and urates dissolve.

Hydrochloric acid:

The human body generates hydrochloric acid, HCl (stomach juice), as needed. There is no reservoir or pouch for hydrochloric acid since it would damage the organ holding it. There is a feedback system that monitors the pH of the stomach to be about 4. When the pH goes higher than that, the cells around the stomach walls generate hydrochloric acid from sodium chloride salt and carbonic acid to maintain the stomach acidity.

$$NaCl + H_2CO_3 = HCl + NaHCO_3$$

As the hydrochloric acid goes into the stomach, sodium bicarbonate is injected into the blood stream. However, when the food from the stomach enters the small intestine, it is too acidic for the intestine to take and exactly the reverse phenomenon takes place. The pancreas injects sodium bicarbonate (known as pancreatic juice) into the small intestine while it sends hydrochloric acid to the blood.

When our blood receives an acidic solution such as hydrochloric acid, we get tired and drowsy. Neutralization of the acid solution by alkaline compounds such as sodium bicarbonate results in a creation of carbonic acid in the blood. It is this carbonic acid that makes you feel lethargic.

We experience sleepiness after a big meal, not during the meal. During the meal, the blood gets sodium bicarbonate and we don't feel tired. It's after the meal when the food moves out from the stomach into the intestine when we feel drowsy, because that's the time when the hydrochloric acid goes into the blood creating carbonic acid, acidifying the blood.

$$HCl + NaHCO_3 = NaCl + H_2CO_3$$

Sodium chloride is an essential salt for our body to function properly. We can use more of sodium to neutralize acidic wastes; however, the remaining part of the sodium chloride, that is, the chlorine is the troublesome factor. If we can supply alkaline minerals such as sodium, calcium and potassium in the form of NaOH, $Ca(OH)_2$ and KOH, that would be the best. Alkaline water gives them!

It was reported in USA Today that the University of California, Berkeley, CA, published a report in 1988 saying that it was not the sodium in sodium chloride that was bad but that the chlorine was detrimental to one's health. They reported that potassium chloride had the same ill effect as sodium chloride. However, it is important to note that the ratio of sodium and potassium is vital in keeping a normal balance of water in the cells and in the extracellular fluids.

In this chapter, our discussion focused on food. However, if you note, I have not said anything about the nutritional values of food nor about the valuable vitamin components of food. There are hundreds of books all about the nutrition and the vitamins found in food. All I have addressed is the *waste products* of the food. The key point of health, longevity, and reverse aging is the management and disposal of these waste products.

All foods give energy and nutrients in order for us to function and grow. Different cultures offer different foods and we all "live". The distinctions between the good foods and the bad foods are the types and the quantities of waste products that those foods generate. The better foods are those that generate the least amount of acidic waste products and the most amount of acid neutralizing byproducts. However, because 97% of our food is carbon, nitrogen, hydrogen, and oxygen and only 3% could be alkaline minerals, no matter what you eat, the waste products are acidic in the final analysis.

If we can help our body to dispose of 100[+] percent of the waste products daily, we can eat any food that we enjoy and still can maintain good health. This is much better than having to worry about what to eat and what not to eat and miss out on some valuable enzymes that exist only in certain kinds of food, etc. Some of the health diets are so complicated that they are very much confusing and they require tremendous will power to stay with. And some diets are boring and unpalatable. I don't recommend over indulgence of any food but I think that forced total abstention of any particular food is much worse.

The important thing to remember in this chapter is the fact that all foods, health or junk, expensive or not, good tasting or bad, produce acidic waste products that our body has to get rid of. And thankfully you don't have to remember all those chemical formulas. In the following chapters we will discuss the disposal of these acidic waste products in order to stay young and healthy.

Chapter 4

The Human Body

4.1) A Survival Machine

The human body is a marvelous survival machine, well engineered by the Creator. Every day, scientists are discovering something new about the way our body works and each discovery adds more appreciation and amazement. There is one simple example that we all can understand and marvel at: the wisdom of the engineering of the human body.

Acidic skin prevents bacteria invasion

Our body is designed to perspire through our skin so that the evaporation of the liquid can cool off our body on a warm day. However, perspiration is not just for the maintenance of body temperature. It protects our body against the invasion of viruses and bacteria. Perspiration is one of the means to dispose of acidic waste products. As such it keeps our skin constantly acid, killing viruses and bacteria.

When we have an operation and the skin is cut open, we are vulnerable to viruses and bacteria. That's why we get infections after an operation or skin cut, not because the hospital is filthier than our home. Bacteria and viruses are continually all around us. It's our built-in immune system that's keeping us healthy and alive. A study of the God-engineered immune system and enhancing the power of that immune system are much better than developing drugs to cure diseases after the illnesses develop.

Influence of electric and magnetic fields

According to Dr. Becker (in his book "The Body Electric"[4]), the regrowth of animal limbs is controlled by an electric field, which he calls the current of injury. Dr. Becker also demonstrated that a human bone has the property of a piezoelectric substance and creates positive or negative electric fields depending upon whether the bone is stretched or compressed. The negative electric field aligns collagen molecules in a direction that builds up the bone to give it more strength.

He also experimented with salamander legs to study the anesthetic effects of the electric field and the electromagnetic field. The important conclusion of his work was that the animal body is greatly influenced by the invisible electric and magnetic fields of the environment. He is concerned about the electromagnetic pollution in the air that may be slowly killing people.

There are helpful electric and magnetic fields and, at the same time, there are harmful fields. The human body generates the fields that are necessary in order to control the growth and regrowth of our body parts.

Immune theory

The Germans claim that the reduction of oxygen within our body lowers the immune power, and they advocate the infusion of oxygen and/or ozone intravenously or rectally. The Japanese say that the reduction of immune power occurs when our body becomes too acidic and they advocate alkaline food and alkaline water. Since more acid means less oxygen (as discussed in chapter 2), the Germans and the Japanese are virtually saying the same thing. However, I believe that the Germans are looking at the symptoms while the Japanese are hitting the causes.

4.2) Disposal System

One thing that everyone can agree upon is that we get tired after a long, vigorous activity that has generated a lot of waste products more rapidly than we can get rid of. We need rest in order to allow our body to dispose of wastes so that we can feel better. When we rest, we discard wastes faster than we generate them. Discarding the acidic wastes means the increase of alkalinity and the increase of oxygen.

Kidneys, lungs, skin, etc.

While we are resting, our blood is busy neutralizing harmful acidic substances and carrying them to the kidneys and lungs. The kidneys remove neutralized waste salts, uric acid, ammonia, etc. while the lungs take carbon dioxide out from carbonic acids making the blood more alkaline. The blood pH is the highest when it comes out of the lungs.

When we talk about the pH of blood, we are talking about the artery blood because this is the blood that comes out of our lungs where the carbon dioxides are removed. The pH of the blood in veins fluctuates depending upon your activities. When the artery blood pH is low, we are in trouble. Artery blood pH of 6.95 can result in a coma and even death.

While resting, we generate minimum amounts of waste products. We still burn nutrients in order to maintain our body temperature even when we are doing absolutely nothing. A far infrared sleeping pad, which will be discussed later on in chapter 6, can help our body maintain this temperature, burning less nutrients.

Our body waste is disposed of chiefly through urine and perspiration. Wastes through bowel movements are the left overs of the foods that our body didn't use. I am not addressing those wastes. The wastes that I am referring to are the ones created in our cells to generate energy, to repair the cells, and to grow. There is a small amount of liquid disposal through the colon also, but it is negligible compared to the liquid disposed of by the kidneys and skin.

Blood, the main carrier

All of the substances in our cells are delivered there by the blood and anything that is removed from the cells must be carried out by the blood. Therefore, these substances must be dissolved in the blood. Once these waste products are brought into the blood, they can be carried to the lungs and to the kidneys in liquid form. If anybody loses weight, say 30 lbs. by a special diet, all of that 30 lbs. of substance comes out via urine and perspiration. That's why one has to drink plenty of water with any diet program.

Doctors don't tell you what kind of water you should be drinking with your diet program. By now you can guess that alkaline water would be better because the wastes that you want to discard are all acidic wastes such as fatty acid, acetic acid, lactic acid, cholesterol, etc. For these acid substances to come out safely, alkaline minerals must be used in your body in order to neutralize them. For that reason, doctors check your blood to make sure that you are not losing too many alkaline minerals.

Alkaline water helps the best

If you drink acid free alkaline water with your diet program, you don't have to worry about losing valuable alkaline minerals. Unfortunately, most American doctors don't know about this acid free high pH alkaline water. How to make this alkaline water will be discussed in chapter 6.

4.3) Homeostasis

In order to sustain human life, the body must maintain a constant body temperature, and constant body fluid pH values such as stomach juice, blood, and pancreatic juice. The process of creating stomach juice and pancreatic juice has been covered in chapter 3. The process of maintaining the blood pH values to within a narrow range of 7.3 to 7.45 is much more complicated.

As I mentioned in chapter 2, a glass of cola with its pH value of 2.5 can change 10 gallons of water with a pH value of 7.4 into water with a 4.6 pH. As we drink highly acidic drinks or as we exercise, the blood becomes acidic instantaneously. The body must act quickly to restore the pH values back to the safe range.

Blood buffers

In our blood plasma, two compounds (one alkaline and one acid) are dissolved, maintaining a certain balance. The alkaline compound is sodium bicarbonate ($NaHCO_3$) and the other is carbonic acid (H_2CO_3). If we increase the amount of carbonic acid, as in when we exercise, the blood becomes more acidic. If that happens, we automatically breath deeply to get rid of CO_2 through the lungs and out, to become less acidic.

Another way the body prevents increased acidity is through alkaline blood buffers such as sodium bicarbonate ($NaHCO_3$) and alkaline sodium phosphate (Na_2HPO_4). The neutralization process using these buffers are as follows.

$$HCl + NaHCO_3 = NaCl + H_2O + CO_2 = NaCl + H_2CO_3$$
$$HCl + Na_2HPO_4 = NaH_2PO_4 + NaCl$$

In the first equation, hydrochloric acid and sodium bicarbonate become salt and carbonic acid. In the second process, hydrochloric acid and alkaline sodium phosphate generate the same salt and acid (dihydrogen) sodium phosphate. It so happens that both the 'alkaline' and the 'acid' sodium phosphate are almost neutral substances.

Wastes that remain

In the first equation above, carbonic acid is volatile; therefore it can be exhaled. However, in the second equation, the acid sodium phosphate, NaH_2PO_4, is non-volatile and therefore cannot be exhaled. Although this type of weak acid saves the blood from becoming strongly acidic by hydrochloric acid, the accumulation of this type of non-volatile acid eventually will tax the kidneys.

If large amounts of non-volatile acid appear in the blood, there is danger that the fixed bases of the blood salts, especially sodium and potassium, may be carried away through the kidneys and thus lost from the body. Acid minerals such as sulfur, phosphorus, chlorine, etc. eventually require alkaline minerals such as potassium, sodium, calcium, magnesium, etc.

Many years of a meat and potato diet with an insufficient amount of vegetables and fruits create acid imbalance and the body gradually becomes more acidic. As we age, the body extracts calcium from the bones to balance the blood and body pH, and the bones become brittle, developing osteoporosis.

Conversion of liquid acid to solid acid

Another trick that the blood plays to prevent sudden acidification is to change liquid acid into undissolved solid acid. Cholesterol and crystallized uric acid are examples of these solidified acids. When high pH alkaline water is consumed, these solid acids become liquid acids bringing down the pH to the normal range. An Insufficient amount of alkaline minerals will build up these solid acids, eventually causing health problems.

4.4) Life Style and Acidification

We live in a highly competitive world. We are constantly on the go, pushing ourselves to the limit. We stay up late to watch the late news and Nightline, yet in the morning we get up early because of our responsibilities. Many of us don't even know how to relax and take it easy. Some takes up sports, but even then they are usually highly competitive sports.

Stress and acid

Stress, whether physical or mental, creates more acid. An ulcer is a good example of that. Under tension, we burn more nutrients in a short amount of time, creating a lot more wastes than the body can dispose of. For this reason, stress speeds up aging. Exercise is a form of stress; one produces more waste products during exercise, but it is usually followed by a resting and relaxation period. The proper amount of exercise followed by a resting period helps get rid of waste products including accumulated waste, especially if one drinks alkaline water during that rest period.

Exercise elevates one's internal body temperature and it expands clogged up capillary vessels. Then the high-temperature blood dissolves old waste products that are "hiding" deep within clogged up capillaries. One may experience a small amount of dizzyness. Too much exercise without rest can develop lactic acid problems which are the results of the incomplete burning of nutrients due to a lack of oxygen.

Mental stress, the worst

Mental stress can be more devastating than physical stress because there is no rest period. One can continue on with mental stress until it can really acidify the person. It is a vicious cycle. Mental stress creates more acids and the acids can make you feel more depressed. Japanese doctors claim that drinking alkaline water can change a depressed mood into a brighter, calmer mood.

Acidic diet and drinks

What about our diets? Meat and potatoes, or oyster and lobster? These days more people are health conscious; however, we still eat more acid forming foods than alkaline forming foods. Some of the so-called health diets are boring and unpalatable. Everything that we like seems to be bad for us, either high in cholesterol, high in sugar, high in sodium, etc.

It is confusing to the point that people just don't care. Some even say that if they have to live without enjoying food, they don't want to live long anyway. What about drinks? It's "the Pepsi Generation" or "Coke is It!" Animals instinctively know what's good for them while people eat or drink whatever the TV tells them to.

End results: storage of acids

What do these lifestyles mean to our body? Well, it all signifies that we are not allowing our body to totally get rid of its acidic waste products. What we don't get rid of, we end up storing somewhere in our body. Since our blood pH cannot be dragged down by these acidic wastes, they must be stored away from the flow of the blood.

We see quite a few people with obesity problems. Exactly what does their excess weight consist of? The answer is fatty acid. When we over-ingest carbohydrates and do not burn them away, they become fatty acid. I stated before that if you rest, your body gets rid of more wastes than it generates; however, the body does not dispose of unburnt food. We can burn this fatty acid 'later' when we need it. To a point it is a reservoir, but 'later' never comes and we keep adding to the reservoir.

Effects of storage of acids

As I mentioned earlier, acid coagulates blood, and there is not much blood flow around fat. Usually the capillaries around the acid accumulation are clogged up. Although there are many exceptions, these fatty acids generally form under the skin especially around the waist line for men and around hips, thighs and breasts for women. Any organs or tissues near the acid accumulation get a smaller supply of blood and can get damaged in the long run.

When you compare the face of a young woman and an older woman, you can see the difference in the build up of fat on the face of the older woman. The skin of the older woman does not receive as much blood as the younger woman, and therefore it loses elasticity and requires more make-up to hide lines and show some color. This build up of fat on the face takes place gradually over a long period of time.

Patience

Any unnatural, instant removal of fat can cause side effects. They may look young, but it doesn't last. Even with a face lift operation, since the acidic condition of the body is still there, the face will become fatty again. I feel sorry for those who remove lines from their faces while the insides remain acidic and old.

The best remedy is to drink alkaline water for a few years, not just to remove facial fat but to reduce the body acid level. (See chapter 6.) Then before you know it, the lines will disappear and the color will come back naturally, without any side effects. Unfortunately, this natural process takes time.

Impatience is characteristic of the American lifestyle. A well-known antacid tablet company advertises that its product works in 4.7 seconds! The old adage is true: good things are worth waiting for. When you are planning to live for 300 years, waiting for a few years for your youth and health to come back is an insignificant amount of time.

True understanding of the process of aging will give you patience and will give you the incentive to drink alkaline water or to do whatever it takes to help your body dispose of acidic wastes slowly and steadily.

Chapter 5

Diseases

5.1) Contagious Diseases and Adult Diseases

The Japanese classify human diseases into two categories: contagious diseases and adult diseases. Contagious diseases are caused by viruses and bacteria, and with the exception of AIDS, modern medical science is very much advanced in taking care of them. In a few years, they will find the cure for AIDS as well, I am sure.

Adult diseases are non-contagious diseases that we develop, just because we get old. Examples of adult diseases are cancer; heart disease, atherosclerosis, high blood pressure; diabetes; arthritis, gout; kidney disease; chronic diarrhea and constipation; hemorrhoids; asthma, hay fever, allergies; headaches, neuralgia; psoriasis, hives, eczema, other skin disorders; hyperacidity, indigestion, gas, nausea, etc.; fever; obesity; tooth and gum diseases; osteoporosis, leg cramps; hangovers; morning sickness.

Common causes of adult diseases

The Japanese claim that the underlying causes of these adult diseases are the accumulation of acids in our body, poor blood circulation and poor cell activity.

Ever since the success of penicillin against the infections caused by invisible bacteria and viruses, medical researchers have been looking for medicine to cure every kind of disease including adult diseases. None of these drugs reduce the acidity of the body. As a matter of a fact, most drugs are acidic.

Since these adult diseases are caused by too much acid in our body, according to the Japanese, unless the treatment actually removes acids from the body, the 'cure' at best will be only temporary. And if the medicine were successful in removing acid from the affected area, the acid would go to some other place in the body to create side effects there, unless the treatment involves the disposal of acids from our body. For this reason, today's medical 'science' is rather poor when it comes to the cure of adult diseases.

5.2) Cancer

The Growth of cancer cells

A German biochemist, Dr. Otto Warburg discovered the 'cause' of cancer back in 1923 and he received the 1931 Nobel Prize for doing so. In his book, "The Metabolism of Tumors"[28], Dr. Warburg demonstrated that the primary cause of cancer was the replacement of *oxygen* in the respiratory chemistry of normal cells by the fermentation of *sugar*. The growth of cancer cells is a fermentation process which can be initiated only in the relative absence of oxygen.

One may wonder how any cell can survive, much less grow, in the absence of oxygen. But it so happens that plant cells are like that. Oxygen is a waste product that they discard. In other words, cancer cells are plant cells that live within an animal. I understand that the National Cancer Institute verified Warburg's theories in the 1950's; however, very little work has been done to determine the causes of a *lack* of oxygen to the human body.

Among American doctors, Dr. Sheldon Saul Hendler is perhaps one of the very few who is advocating oxygen deficiency as the causes of many illnesses. In his book, entitled "The Oxygen Breakthrough, 30 Days to an Illness-Free Life"[15], Dr. Hendler teaches breathing exercises and oxygen rich diets to overcome the oxygen deficiency problems.

Ever since Warburg's discovery, researchers have been attempting to stop the fermentation process through drugs, radiation and surgery, which, in some cases, have been temporarily successful. In the meantime, the Germans are trying to find ways of getting more oxygen to all of the healthy cells in order to prevent the initiation of the fermentation process.

Oxygen therapies

There are devices and methods available for the purpose of supplying more oxygen to the cells. "O_2xygen Therapies" by Ed McCabe[18] describes a hydrogen peroxide (H_2O_2) and ozone (O_3) treatments. Drinking a diluted hydrogen peroxide solution or injecting ozone intravenously or rectally will place extra oxygen in the blood through a path other than the lungs.

Recently we are learning that doctors in Europe have long been making use of the body's 'third lung', the colon, during surgery due to its ability to absorb up to 70% of the oxygen introduced to it.

Although I heard a doctor claim to have destroyed 80% of a breast tumor by directly injecting ozone into the tumor, I question the validity of this kind of oxygen treatment **unless** the patient had a respiratory problem and was not able to breath in oxygen through the lungs. Oxygen infused in this manner eventually dissipates and it does not convert the acidic environment to an alkaline one.

The true cause of cancer

Herman Aihara, in his book entitled "Acid & Alkaline"[1], states that:

> "If the condition of our extracellular fluids, especially the blood, becomes acidic, our physical condition will first manifest tiredness, proneness to catching colds, etc. When these fluids become more acidic, our condition then manifests pains and suffering such as headaches, chest pains, stomach aches, etc. According to Keiichi Morishita in his *Hidden Truth of Cancer*, if the blood develops a more acidic condition, then our body inevitably deposits these excess acidic substances in some area of the body such so that the blood will be able to maintain an alkaline condition.
>
> As this tendency continues, such areas increase in acidity and some cells die; then these dead cells themselves turn into acids. However, some other cells may adapt in that environment. In other words, instead of dying - as normal cells do in an acid environment - some cells survive by becoming abnormal cells. These abnormal cells are called malignant cells. Malignant cells do not correspond with brain function nor with our own DNA memory code. Therefore, malignant cells grow indefinitely and without order. This is cancer."

In chapter 2, I showed the relationship between alkalinity and excess oxygen in water. Mr. Aihara does not mention anything about the lack of oxygen but rather talks about the acidification of extra cellular fluids which causes cancer. Dr. Warburg states that the primary cause of cancer is the lack of oxygen in a cell, like a plant cell. He didn't know what caused the lack of oxygen.

I think Dr. Warburg was dealing with the symptom of acid build ups rather than the cause. Mr. Aihara was hitting the nail right on the head. For this reason, the German solution is to alleviate the symptoms, that is, to supply more oxygen, while the Japanese solution is to reduce the acidity, the very cause, by alkaline diet and/or alkaline water.

Alkaline therapies

When you drink alkaline water, you are drinking water with excess oxygen, not in the form of O_2, but in the form of OH^- which is very stable because it is mated with positively ionized alkaline minerals. Two of these hydroxyl ions can form a water molecule (H_2O) and give out one oxygen atom. The alkaline mineral is used to detoxify poisonous acid compounds and when that happens the hydroxyl ion is freed to supply excess oxygen to the cells to prevent the development of cancer. It is indeed the case of killing two birds with one stone.

We are talking about two kinds of oxygen. One is in a dynamic form, O_2, and the other is in the stable bias form of OH^- mated with positively ionized alkaline minerals. The body needs both kinds of oxygen. If you hold your breath, O_2 is cut off and you die, and if your body pH goes down below 7, OH^- is cut off and you would die also. When breathing stops, O_2 is first used up and the body will use up OH^- secondly, then death will occur. That takes about three minutes. Those people with high alkalinity, like babies, would live longer than 3 minutes.

Reflecting back on the research works done by the two scientists, what is happening in our body may be as follows. When the environment for the cells becomes too acidic, there isn't enough oxygen to go around for all the cells in the area. In order for some cells to survive under the circumstances, they selectively change some cells to plant cells so that they can take in CO_2 and give out O_2. The convenience of the moment may cause damage later on, but at least it caused the survival of life for a little longer.

Remember, the human body is a marvelously engineered survival machine.

Conventional medical therapies

Today's medical industry treats malignant cells as if they were bacteria or viruses. They try to destroy them at any cost and usually the cost is the immune system of the patient. Since malignant cells are derived from healthy cells, trying to destroy one will affect the other. Chemotherapy or radiation treatments may be able to destroy 'all' of the malignant cells, but by that time the healthy cells are damaged to the point that they cannot destroy simple everyday bacteria and that person can lose his life.

Surgery for a malignant tumor is perhaps more selective. However, even after 'successful' surgery where 'all' of the tumors were removed, they can recur because the acidic environment has not been changed to an alkaline one. Radiation treatment after the surgery is another mistake. It will destroy some healthy cells and when those cells die, they become acidic wastes. A shot of sodium bicarbonate may be much better than radiation treatment, provided that a proper ratio of sodium and potassium is maintained.

It is discouraging to see that cancer research is divided into so many specialties such as cancer of the liver, cervical cancer, cancer of the kidneys, cancer of the pancreas, etc. The cause of all cancer is a lack of oxygen caused by acidification. But when so many doctors are specializing cancer research in such narrow fields, they will never find the true overall picture. They will be forever lost in a maze.

Best cancer prevention means

Drinking high pH alkaline water will definitely help in preventing cancer. Research should be done by the National Cancer Institute to see how alkaline water may help in curing early stages of cancer, depending upon how far the cancer has progressed. I am sure that there is a point of no return. However, since the healthy cells are alkaline and the malignant cells are acidic, drinking alkaline water will not harm healthy cells while it may destroy malignant cells. It is worth trying.

5.3) Heart Disease, Atherosclerosis, High Blood Pressure

Your blood is your body's transport system. It carries both nutrients and oxygen to the tissues of your body. It also carries waste products away from the tissues and helps maintain body temperature. To do these things, your blood must circulate continuously. Your heart is the center of the circulation and it pumps over 5 quarts of blood every minute.

Acidification of the body starts in the blood. As mentioned before, the blood performs a balancing acts in order to maintain the blood pH within the safe range of 7.3 to 7.45. The blood has a buffer pool of sodium bicarbonate made to neutralize strong acid compounds coming out of the cells as waste products of metabolism. When this buffer level is too low, acidosis is developed.

Acidosis and high blood pressure

Dr. Kancho Kuninaka, one of the pioneers of the alkaline water treatment in Japan, states that virtually without exception, the patients with high blood pressure have an acidosis condition.[25] He has many successful clinical cases where the acid free high pH alkaline water lowered blood pressure.

There are several plausible explanations for this phenomenon. Since the higher pH blood contains excess oxygen, the heart doesn't have to work as hard. Another factor may be that the viscosity of the higher pH blood is low so that the heart does not need to pump as hard. A further reason may be that the calcium ions in alkaline water may be dissolving plaque and cholesterol build-up in the artery walls, thus opening up the passage.

Doctors know that if you take several deep breaths right before the blood pressure measurement, you can get a lower reading. You have temporarily elevated the pH of the blood by breathing out more CO_2 and by breathing in more O_2. If you can lower your blood pressure by using this trick, your high blood pressure is caused by the first two reasons in the above paragraph and you should be able to lower your blood pressure within a few months of drinking the alkaline water.

Alkaline water therapies

The above example is the case where your blood pressure fluctuates between high and low. However, if your blood pressure is always high, chances are that your arteries are getting narrow (atherosclerosis) and it will take a long time, possibly a year or more, for that blood pressure to come down by means of alkaline water. It takes time to dissolve plaque and cholesterol build-up, but eventually it will work. This slow process has no side effects. It lowers the blood pressure by eliminating the very causes of the high blood pressure.

Pill therapies

The blood pressure pills are designed to fool your body by chemical means in order to force the blood pressure down. That is why every blood pressure pill has side effects. Unless you are lowering the acid level in the blood, which is the real cause of the high blood pressure, everything else is going to be more harmful and you have to take the pills for the rest of your life. Remember that the blood pressure is high because your body, the marvelously engineered survival machine, is trying to compensate for some deficiency in your body.

Blood pressure and smoking

A friend of mine in Tampa, Florida was telling me about her peculiar blood pressure problem. She was having to go to her doctor's office several times a week to measure her blood pressure. She was taking the blood pressure pills but wanted to cut them out, and her doctor wanted to make sure that it was alright to do so.

The peculiar part of her problem was that at the end of a hectic day at the office, she would be sure of the high pressure, but her blood pressure measured normal. But during the weekend when she had been relaxing at home, watching TV and reading books, her blood pressure measured alarmingly high, so high that the nurse had to call the doctor in.

As she was telling me this story, I made the observation that she smoked. So I told her that the fact that her blood pressure went up and down indicated to me that her problem may be caused by the oxygen level in her blood going up and down. Then I told her that her smoking will lower the oxygen level in her blood.

She looked at me with wide eyes and said: "You know, Sang? We are not allowed to smoke in our office!" Her definition of relaxing at home meant smoking and watching TV, etc. I told her that she didn't have a blood pressure problem but that she had a smoking problem. She said that she would have to work on that.

Blood pressure and sugar

For people with hypertension, doctors advise them not to eat too much fatty food, to cut out meat, to eliminate sugar, and to stop smoking. They should add "cut out soft drinks" to that list. The riddle is: What are the commonalities of all these things? The answer is that they all rob your body of oxygen. Smoking not only reduces the available oxygen from your body but the nicotine has the effect of narrowing capillary vessels. We know by now that all of the acidic foods and drinks lower your blood oxygen level. But what about sugar?

Sugar grabs oxygen with the highest priority. Mr. Gregory Grosbard of Miami, FL received a U.S. patent on improving plastic strength by using sugar. Each time plastic material goes through a heat cycle it loses strength, because oxygen in the atmosphere goes into the material under heat, creating oxygen "holes". As Mr. Grosbard mixed a small amount of sugar into the plastic material during the heat cycle, the sugar grabbed the oxygen first, making the plastic stronger.

Effects of soft drinks

Soft drinks, especially the cola type, are highly acidic. A dentist friend of mine told me that he can demonstrate the tooth decay process by submerging an extracted tooth into a glass of cola and watching it decay. In chapter 2, I calculated that in order to neutralize a glass of cola with a pH of 2.5, it would take 32 glasses of alkaline water with a pH of 10. A 10 oz glass of cola took away 160×10^{20} (16 billion times trillion) oxygen from 32 glasses of alkaline water.

Soft drinks are slow killers. It would be an interesting experiment to test the effects of alkaline water and soft drinks on laboratory mice. If we had three groups of mice evenly grouped as to their age and health condition and we gave one group of mice only cola type drinks; the second, distilled water; and the third, alkaline water, what would be the outcome? We can all guess as to which group would live the longest and which group would end up with the shortest lives.

Lately we have been alarmed by the incidence of younger people being hit by the so-called adult diseases which used to converge mainly on the 40-plus age group. I wouldn't be surprised if the frequency of these incidents are paralleled by the success and the growth of many soft drink companies.

The acidity of some soft drinks is caused by carbon dioxide, which is not so bad because we can eventually breath it out. But some soft drinks are highly acidic even after the carbon dioxide is all fizzled out. Perhaps the consumer advocates group should demand the acidity of the drinks to be clearly indicated on the labels of these soft drinks.

5.4) Diabetes

In a healthy body, the pancreas produces insulin and the insulin manages and helps the body to use sugar and carbohydrates properly. The adult disease diabetes is called *insulin-independent diabetes mellitus*. The Family Medical Guide[2] by the AMA defines it as follows:

> "Insulin-independent diabetes: In this form of diabetes mellitus, which usually affects people over 40, the insulin-producing cells in your pancreas function, but the output of insulin is inadequate for your body's needs. People who have this form of the disorder usually eat too much and are overweight. Their over-eating causes an excess of glucose in their blood, and the pancreas cannot produce enough insulin to cope with it. Heredity is also an important factor. In nearly a third of all cases, there is family history of the malady. Age is also a factor, because the efficiency of your pancreas decreases with age."

Alkaline water therapies

Dr. Keijiro Kuwabara of Japan has been clinically treating diabetes quite successfully by use of alkaline water. He reports[25] that a 49 year old insurance company employee was diagnosed by the company physician as having a case of insulin-independent diabetes mellitus. With only one month's use of alkaline water, the sugar count came down to virtually an undetectable level, from 300mg/dl one month previously.

The pancreas produces one of the highest pH body fluids, pancreatic juice, with its pH value of 8.8. A shortage of calcium ions in the body impairs the production and the release of the insulin hormone. This eventually leads to an acidic blood condition. Clogged blood vessels caused by excess protein buildup also impairs pancreatic function. Alkaline water, by supplying calcium in an ionized form and by helping prevent excess protein buildup, can help prevent and heal this condition.

As we age (by now we know this statement to mean "as we accumulate acidic waste products"), they say, that the efficiency of our pancreas decreases. Apparently we accumulate acidic waste products around the pancreas, men more so than women. Men initially begin to build up fatty acids around the waist.

Adult diseases and heredity

Heredity here may mean that somehow in that particular family, there is a tendency to accumulate waste products at or near the pancreas first. Until they reach 40, the amount of acid accumulation is not sufficient enough to slow down the functions of the pancreas. This means that if we prevent wastes from accumulating by means of alkaline water, that person will not get diabetes even if he reaches 70 or 80 years old.

After all, he didn't have diabetes when he was 30 years old; that is, he didn't have enough of an acidic waste buildup until that time. Chronologically he may reach 40 or 50, but if he can keep the level of the wastes to that of 30 years old, he will never get diabetes. Heredity may not have to be related to chronological age.

The alkaline water treatment will not apply to diabetes of different causes such as a damaged pancreas, etc.

5.5) Arthritis, gout

Many different forms of arthritis and gout are the result of acid accumulation in the joints. Heavy people add more pressure on their joints, thus speeding up wear and tear; however, a young person seems to do fine even if he is heavy. It is the accumulated acid that damages cartilages and irritates the joints. Unfortunately, the joints are where the blood cannot carry out wastes easily.

Gout is the accumulation of uric acid in the joints. According to Webster, gout is a disease resulting from a disturbance of metabolism, characterized by an excess of uric acid in the blood and deposits of uric acid salts in the tissues around the joints, especially of the feet and hands: it causes swelling and severe pain, especially in the big toe.

In today's medicine, there is no effective treatment for these types of degenerative diseases. Because it is painful, one instinctively takes pain killers; however, aspirin types are acidic and they can further irritate the joints. The sooner we accept the fact that these diseases are the result of too much acidic waste, the sooner we will find the cure for these problems.

Cover-up with ointment or remove the cause

These days, pain killing ointments for arthritis are advertized. This is only a temporary cover-up. Lately doctors also advise a change in diet. This is a step in the right direction. Drinking alkaline water will change the acidic condition so that the body will be able to fix the problems by itself.

Mrs. Ginny Sirhal of Fort Lauderdale, Florida wrote me:

"Dear Mr. Whang;

With the water situation as it is today, both my husband and myself, at our ages, are most concerned. (65 & 69)

We installed the best filter on the market several years ago; however, after reading up on what the Super Ion-Q water ionizer does in removing all toxins from one's system, I ordered one, Oct. 1987. So we have used this machine for almost 6 months.

My husband has high uric acid and is a diabetic which causes gouty arthritis. His hands, fingers, knees, actually all of his joints caused him great pain, preventing him from playing golf and some times even getting around. Now he is mainly free of pain which he feels is all due to his drinking the ionized water. He claims he can't live without it.

I, on the other hand, have hypertension, high blood pressure. I swear by this water. My coffee tastes better, cocktails taste better and I feel better. Amy, my 12 year old grand daughter has completely cleared her face of pimples by using the astringent side on the face daily. It's like magic.

This machine, I would guarantee any one, will keep them healthy and out of the doctor's office. It's fantastic and a treasured machine in our kitchen."

Degenerative diseases

In general, degenerative diseases are the results of acid waste buildups within us. When we are born, we have the highest alkaline mineral concentration and also the highest body pH. From that point on, the normal process of life is to gradually acidify. That is why these degenerative diseases do not occur when you are young. They occur usually after 40. The difference between the 20 year old you and the 40 year old you physically is that you have accumulated more acidic wastes at 40 than at 20.

As long as doctors don't accept this fact and look for medicine to treat these degenerative diseases, they will not succeed. They know that a change in diet will help, but it's too time-consuming for them and for their patients, too.

What I am hoping is that the efforts for reverse aging will naturally improve all of these degenerative adult diseases as byproducts or good side effects!

5.6) Kidney Disease

As the body produces more acidic wastes, the kidneys get more taxed because they have to take those acids out from the blood. Nephritis, uremic poisoning, bladder diseases, etc. are all acid-related conditions which can be improved by the consumption of alkaline water. It also helps control osmotic pressure in the kidneys.

Kidney stones

Kidney stones are formed in the kidneys, originally starting as tiny specks of solid substance. As more material clings to the first speck, it gradually builds into a solid object. The substances are made out of phosphates, urates, etc. They are salts of phosphoric acid and uric acid generally combined with calcium and/or magnesium. They are formed in the kidneys because the environment is too acidic. These salts are acidic salts.

Although calcium and magnesium are in the salts, they are there to soften the poisonous effects of uric acid and phosphoric acid. Some people mistakenly believe that kidney stones are formed because there is too much calcium. That is not true. The best proof is that the calcium compound will dissolve in acidic urine while kidney stones will not.

If you add calcium into the bladder and lower the acidity of the urine, kidney stones will dissolve. Drinking plenty of alkaline water will prevent the kidney stones from forming to begin with, and even after the formation, it can dissolve them. Because urine is acidic and so are most of the other waste products, any extra calcium that your body doesn't need will be dissolved and discarded by the urine. In the process, it will help dissolve kidney stones, if any. There is no need to worry about too much calcium consumption.

5.7) Chronic diarrhea and constipation

It sounds like a contradicting statement, but both of these seemingly opposite phenomenon are the result of too many acids. If too much acid affects the pancreatic juice causing it to be less alkaline and the foods coming into the intestine become too acidic, this will cause diarrhea. Alkaline water will help in this case. Relief of constipation is a little harder to understand.

Dr. Kyuwan Choi, Professor of Internal Medicine, Seoul University, conducted a clinical experiment involving 15 patients with a chronic constipation problem. (They had this problem for at least one year.)   Dr. Choi's experiment constituted the measurement of the food passage time through the large intestine, before and after the drinking of alkaline water.

At the Health and Water symposium held in Seoul last Sept. 22, 1989, Dr. Choi reported his findings.[9] Everyone was asked to drink 1.5 liters of alkaline water a day. The following data was taken at the beginning of the experiment and after one week.

Age span of the subjects		39 to 62	years old
Total passage time	: before	45 to 136	hours
	: after	3.1 to 73	hours
Average passage time	: before	74	hours
	: after	40	hours
% reduction time		6.9 to 88.8	%
Average % reduction		51	%

Another finding was that within 1 to 2 weeks everyone made bowel movements once a day. Dr. Choi states that he does not quite understand the reason why it works. From the results shown above, one could conclude that constipation is caused by acid accumulation somewhere near the colon. It is possible that the alkaline water helps the secretion of fluids into the colon by eliminating acid build-up.

5.8) Other Adult Diseases

Asthma, hay fever, allergies

Allergies, in general, are the result of a misguided immune system building up antibodies against normally harmless substances. Asthma is a class of allergies where the allergic reaction results in partial obstruction of the bronchi and bronchiole by contraction of the muscles in the bronchial walls.

They are triggered by pollen, dust, hairs on cats or dogs, or even by moods. Doctors don't know why these things happen to some people. Japanese doctors blame it on the immune disorder caused by acidosis.

I have a friend in Phoenix, AZ who loves to dance. She had to slow down her dancing activities because of the condition that her doctor diagnosed as "exercised-induced asthma". About one hour into her dancing exercise, she used to get attacks. I advised her to drink alkaline water on a regular basis. A couple of months later, I got a call from her saying that her asthma attack was gone!

It is said that asthma cannot be cured, but that an attack can be relieved by treatment. My doctor told me, when he prescribed my blood pressure pills, that I would have to take these pills for the rest of my life! Four years later, I made a liar out of him by drinking alkaline water for just six weeks.

I think that Japanese doctors are correct in assuming that any disease that is not caused by bacteria or viruses is caused by too much acid in the body. When doctors say that they don't know the cause, chances are that it is acid. Somehow American doctors are not looking into the properties of acid and alkaline. In the orient people are always looking at the balance of yin and yang, minus and plus, and acid and alkaline.

Hyperacidity, indigestion, gas, nausea, etc.

All of these symptoms are again caused by too much acid. Suppression of acid by means of alkaline water will help to alleviate and prevent these acid-related intestinal and stomach disorders including ulcers.

For these symptoms we take Alkaseltzer, which is an alkaline drink with carbon dioxide fizzles added to it. I guess the carbon dioxide fizzles are added because the taste is quite bitter.

Osteoporosis

The skeletal structure of the body is a "calcium bank". When the body's condition becomes too acidic, it frequently makes compensating withdrawals of calcium from the bones, leaving them brittle and subject to breakage. A bone is made out of proper combinations of calcium and phosphorus. When just the calcium is removed, the remaining bone becomes highly phosphorus and it becomes weak.

The postures of many old people change and they seem to get shorter as they age. These are the results of losing calcium from the skeletal structure. Prolonged usage of alkaline water can help prevent this disaster of the modern diet. Ionized calcium can help to repair the damages.

Morning sickness

When a woman gets pregnant, the fetus takes priority in getting all the necessary alkaline minerals, since a baby is born with the highest alkalinity. This means that while she is sleeping, she loses a lot of alkaline minerals and her blood becomes acidic rather suddenly. According to Japanese doctors, this phenomenon is known as morning sickness.

It was after my daughter and daughter-in-law got pregnant that I was able to confirm this statement. The first thing that they looked for in the morning was alkaline water. Among the effects of drinking alkaline water, perhaps this phenomenon shows the most dramatic visible result. Pregnant women lose a lot of alkaline minerals. Mineral supplements and the continued ingestion of alkaline water are recommended.

Eye diseases

We generally do not consider the change in our vision as we age to be any kind of disease. We consider that to be a sign of aging and accept it as a fact of life. However, how or why do these things happen? Undoubtedly, the process of acidification does something.

As we accumulate phosphates and urates etc. in our cells, the cells lose more oxygen. This causes more unburned sugar in the cell that will bond protein molecules. The end result is that the cells and tissues get stiff, inflexible, hard, etc.

If we do not allow the acids to accumulate in our cells, these things would not have to happen. Then the next question is "Can we reverse it?" I don't have many examples but for two out of two, the answer is yes!

Up until I was 40 years old, I didn't need any glasses. Slowly my eyesight worsened, and by the time I was 55 years old, I was wearing glasses. For distance, I needed a plano with one diopter astigmatism. For reading, I had to add 1.5 diopter. Because of my astigmatism, I needed glasses to drive. I had to have prescription sun glasses.

In one of my trips to New York a couple of years ago, I lost my glasses. Arriving back to Miami at night, I wondered how I could drive back home. I had no choice but to drive without glasses. That's when I made an incredible realization. I didn't need my glasses! I never reordered glasses after that.

For reading I bought non prescription reading glasses from the drug store. I tried +1.5 diopter reading glasses. The prescription was too strong. I settled with +1.25 diopter, which was the weakest add power reading glasses that I could buy. Today I know that I can use +1.00 diopter reading glasses but drug stores do not have them.

My wife Mary is nearsighted. The glasses that she wore for the past 3 years had -6.00 diopters for distance with 1 diopter astigmatism. Her adds for reading were about +2.00 diopter. Recently she was having problems seeing with her glasses. Since the experiences she had with her glasses were that every few years she had to get stronger prescriptions, she thought that she needed a stronger prescription. She found her old pair of glasses and tried that on for testing. She was surprised to find that the old pair was much better.

We went to an optometrist nearby and got a new prescription for Mary. Her new prescription was -5.00 for distance with .75 diopter astigmatism and her adds for reading were +2.00 diopters. When I explained to the doctor about my reverse aging theory and that the elimination of old wastes from the cells and tissues might be making her eye sight improve, he was a little skeptical.

He said that myopia doesn't get better as one gets older. He suspected that the previous doctor who prescribed Mary's glasses may have made a mistake and over-compensated. But he said: "If you come back in a couple of years and her prescription changes to -4.00 diopters, then you've got something." The fact is that Mary has been using this pair for over 3 years without any problem.

I don't know about other people, but I do know that my wife and I drink alkaline water everyday and that she uses this water for cooking everything. We have been drinking alkaline water for almost 4 years and every once in a while we discover some more unexpected changes for the better.

5.9) Contagious diseases

Although contagious diseases are not caused by acid accumulation, the consumers of alkaline water claim that their immunity against these diseases is high, so they do not get sick very often. But even if one does get sick, the recovery period is fairly rapid.

The Japanese claim that increased alkalinity means higher immunity against contagious diseases and the Germans claim that an increased oxygen level signifies higher immunity.

When the body is invaded by foreign bacteria or viruses, white blood cells declare war against the invaders. This war creates casualties on both sides. Those casualties are dead cells, and they are acidic. For this reason, a person with more alkaline minerals can dispose of these acidic wastes quickly and recover more rapidly. We know very well that a bout with flu drains alkaline minerals and that doctors tell us to eat bananas to replace lost potassium.

Edgar Cayce's prediction

Over a half century ago, the world's most renowned psychic, Edgar Cayce, spoke out against any carbonated drinks. And for a 36 year old man with neuritis (tendencies, acidity), Mr. Cayce speaks 'in trance': ... "Also more water in the system, systematically taken that the acid in the system may be dissolved."[6] (2/28/1924 779-6)

On July 12, 1935, Mr. Cayce was asked and answered the following question in trance.

"Q. Can immunization against contagious diseases be set up in any other manner than by inoculations?

A. If an alkalinity is maintained in the system - especially with the lettuce, carrots and celery, these in the blood supply will maintain such a condition as to immunize a person. In an alkaline system there is less effect of cold and congestion."

Twentieth century science is catching up with Mr. Cayce half a century later.

Chapter 6

Reverse Aging Methods and Devices

All foods create waste products within our cells and tissues after metabolism, and our life styles do not allow our body to dispose of these waste products completely. The accumulation of these leftover waste products is the aging process. Therefore, reverse aging is the process of discharging old accumulated waste products out from our body.

As it was discussed in chapter 3, these waste products are acidic, and therefore our body gradually gets more acidic as a result. Reverse aging requires two separate steps: chemical and physical.

The first step is to lower the acidity of the body so that it can dispose of acidic wastes in the blood and cellular fluids safely and easily. The second step is to physically pull out old stored wastes into the blood stream so that they can be discharged from the body.

There are several ways to achieve reverse aging. Some we already know and some are rather new to us but are much easier than the known methods. The known methods are an alkaline diet (vegetarian diet, macrobiotic diet, etc.), which is chemical, and exercise, which is physical.

6.1) Chemical Attack

Since the basic problem is too much acid, the solution is to put in alkaline minerals. There are many reference books available which list mineral contents in our ordinary food.[1,7,11] Most of the health food stores carry them. Unfortunately, different reference books do not agree on everything, and I must admit that they can be confusing.

For example, they say that brown rice is healthier than white rice. However, 1 cup of brown rice contains 608 mg of phosphorus, an acid mineral, and 1 cup of white rice contains only 258 mg of phosphorus, according to Ms. Adelle Davis.[11] The macrobiotic diet promotes brown rice. Many foods high in calcium contain large amounts of phosphorus also.

Sifting through many tables and charts, one can come up with some basic rules. Although there are exceptions, vegetables and fruits in general are alkaline forming foods, and grains and meats including chicken and fish are acid forming foods. Remember that we are talking about what the residue ash does to our body and not how it tastes.

Acid forming foods

Among the foods that we are familiar with (since these macrobiotic reference books are developed in Japan, there are many foods that are unfamiliar to us), the acid forming foods are as follows, in order of acidity: rice bran, egg yolk, oatmeal, brown rice, tuna, chicken, carp, bream, oysters, salmon, buckwheat flour, clams, scallops, pork, peanuts, herring eggs, beef, cheese, whole barley, shrimp, peas, beer, bread, chicken soup, butter, and asparagus. (From a table by Aihara[1])

We hear so much about beef being bad, but chicken, tuna and egg yolk are 2, 3 and 4 times more acid forming than beef. And beef has special enzymes that our body needs which we cannot get from any other food. (The Beef Industry Council should love this book.)

Alkaline forming food

The alkaline forming foods are as follows, in order of alkalinity: ginger, kidney beans, spinach, soybeans, bananas, chestnuts, carrots, mushrooms, strawberries, potatoes, cabbage, radishes, squash, bamboo shoots, sweet potatoes, turnips, orange juice, apples, egg white, pears, grape juice, cucumbers, watermelons, eggplants, coffee, onions, tea, string beans, human milk, cow's milk, and tofu (bean curd). (From the same table by Aihara[1])

Balanced & mixed diet in moderation

There are many Americans who are following vegetarian diets or macrobiotic diets, trying to reduce the acidity of the body. However, it is not easy for most of us. I believe in a balanced diet and everything in moderation. All food tastes different and each has a unique element within it that is difficult to get from other food sources. Therefore, exclusion of any particular food may create some deficiency.

Not all food is just burned to get energy. Some food is reduced to small-sized molecules and used to build or repair our body. Even if we don't know, the body knows what it needs, and selectively picks out what is necessary. What the body does not take becomes waste products. We eat far more food than the minimum required to sustain our life. Since we don't know exactly what the body needs, eat all kinds of food and let your intelligent body pick out what it needs.

Drinking alkaline water

What I am advocating is that we shouldn't use food to discard waste products but instead use water to wash out the wastes. Enjoy a variety of foods in moderation and drink the right kind of water to dispose of all of the waste products. Since the waste products that we are trying to discharge are acidic, the right kind of water is alkaline water.

A glass of alkaline water (10 oz.) with a pH of 10 contains 10^{21} hydroxyl ions (OH-) and each one of them are mated with positively ionized alkaline minerals such as Ca^{++}, Mg^{++}, Na^+, K^+, etc. Since there is more calcium in the water than any other alkaline mineral, if we assume that every ionized mineral was calcium, it translates into 33.3 mgs of *ionized* calcium atoms in that glass.

Drinking 5 glasses of this water daily will gradually lower the body's acidity and enable the body to dispose of all the waste products produced daily and **then** some. Drinking ionized alkaline water is much better than taking alkaline mineral tablets such as calcium tablets.

Mineral supplements

Calcium tablets sold in stores are not in the form of pure calcium, but they are neutral compounds with some other substances. First they must be dissolved and then ionized to be effective. Only a part of the compound actually gets dissolved and ionized. For example, when a calcium carbonate compound is dissolved and ionized in water it breaks up as Ca^{++} and CO_3^{--}, and forms $Ca(OH)_2$ and H_2CO_3. Calcium hydroxide $Ca(OH)_2$ is the same form of calcium in alkaline water, but this solution contains carbonic acid H_2CO_3 which the lungs must breath out.

When any "pure" alkaline minerals such as K, Na, Ca, Mg, etc. are put in water, they will "boil" water rather rapidly. What happens is that these minerals will kick one hydrogen atom out of a water molecule to form KOH, NaOH, $Ca(OH)_2$, and $Mg(OH)_2$. The hydrogen atoms that are kicked out combine two by two to become hydrogen molecules H_2 and bubble up as if the water is boiling.

If you put any calcium tablet into water and you don't see the water "boiling", the calcium is not "pure", even if the bottle says that it is pure calcium. Pure potassium in water reacts so vigorously that it almost looks like an explosion.

How to make this alkaline water from your tap water will be discussed in section 6.3.

6.2) Physical Attack

As mentioned before, acid coagulates blood. As a result, capillary vessels get clogged up close to where the acid wastes accumulate deep within your body. This means that even if the blood gets more alkaline, it cannot reach the acidic wastes. Alkaline effects can reach them through osmosis but this is a slower process.

For the blood to reach the acid pile quickly, you have to elevate the internal temperature of the body to expand the capillary vessels. Then the warm blood can not only reach the acid pile but also dissolve it better into the blood because the blood is warmer. You see, warm water washes dishes better than cold water.

Usually, older waste products are surrounded by clogged up capillary vessels. If you can reach waste products that are 10 years old and get rid of them, you are literally getting 10 years younger.

THIS IS REVERSE AGING!

There are many ways to elevate the internal temperature of our body.

Exercise

The one that doctors recommend is EXERCISE! Exercise provides many benefits such as toning muscles, burning off calories, etc.

Another one of the benefits of exercise is to elevate the body's internal temperature and to expand clogged up capillary vessels in order to suck out old wastes or fat that you have stored for later use.

Yes, exercise creates more acidic wastes, but for reaching and getting rid of old wastes, there is net gain. If you over-exercise without resting, you create lactic acid from exercising and drag out old acidic wastes into your blood, making your blood highly acidic. That's why sometimes you feel dizzy and faint during exercise. Often we hear the term "exercise-induced asthma". A sudden increase of acid in the blood will do that. Drinking alkaline water will help.

Hot bath, sauna, massage, fasting, etc.

Another method of elevating internal temperature is to take a hot bath, or get into a hot sauna. Here again you feel dizzy and faint afterwards because the toxic acid wastes are getting into your blood. A massage can squeeze out old wastes too. The massaged area warms up as well. I have seen a far infrared sauna where the chamber temperature is only 40°C (104°F), but once you go inside, your body feels warm because the far infrared waves penetrate deeply, and you perspire quite a bit. This kind of sauna is good for a person with a weak heart.

Fasting is another method to extract old accumulated wastes. In an effort to survive in the absence of incoming food, the body looks for stored fat for energy. Stored with the fat are other acid toxins and dead cells which are acidic. The waste products generated during fasting are much more acidic than during normal time. This means that there is a great risk of losing valuable body alkaline minerals. One should drink an ample amount of alkaline water.

Far infrared sleeping pad

The device that I like the best for elevating internal body temperature to melt away old waste products is a "far infrared sleeping pad". It is a couple of inches thick, designed to put on top of a firm mattress or on the floor. Far infrared waves are generated by passing a DC current through a carbon impregnated cotton sheet. You can adjust the temperature to your liking.

It is different from an ordinary electric heating pad. The surface is not warm to the touch, but when you lie down on it, you feel warm on the inside. Later on, your body adapts to the temperature and burns less nutrients in order to maintain body temperature, yet it heats you on the inside to melt away those acidic wastes. During the first few weeks of use, one sometimes experiences dizziness when waking up in the morning, a phenomena that is similar to the feeling you get when you take a hot bath. This concerns some people that it might be a bad side effect. But this is actually a sign that the pad is working.

Since it is not a 60 cycle AC current running in the wire, there are no 60 cycle induced currents in your body as with an electric blanket. Since an electric blanket heats you by means of conduction, the surface must be very hot to warm you on the inside as much as the far infrared pad does. It does this by deeply penetrating radiation means like microwaves, but it is a safe spectrum. More about the new revolutionary far infrared waves in detail in section 6.4.

The reason why I like this far infrared sleeping pad the best is that it requires no special effort. Other methods, such as exercising, taking a hot bath, having a massage done, doing a sauna, etc. require special time out to do and our life style makes it very difficult to continue on for more than 6 months. However, no matter how busy you are, or how lazy you are, you do sleep! It requires no special effort.

Disabled people and very old people cannot exercise, and there are some areas of our body that we don't even know how to exercise. But once you own this pad, anybody can use it and get the benefits of reverse aging.

6.3) Alkaline Water Maker

6.3.1) History of the Water Ionizer[24]

Alkaline water is made by a water ionizer by electrically splitting filtered tap water into alkaline water and acid water. This ionizer was first developed in Japan in the early 50's, and the experiments were first conducted on plants and animals. Full scale development started in 1954 by several Japanese agricultural universities on the effects of ionized water, especially acid water, on plants. Today, nursery farmers that supply cut flowers use acid water to keep flowers fresh longer before delivery to the flower shops.

Experiments on the human body took much longer because of the difficulties in maintaining the constancy of the environments. Nevertheless, through long, patient experiments by the medical doctors in Japan, much valuable data has been collected and it was concluded that alkaline water made by the water ionizer was non-toxic and alleviated many symptoms of adult diseases.

The first commercial water ionizers were available in Japan in 1958. Until then, the only water ionizers available were large units used in hospitals. In 1960, a group of medical doctors and agricultural doctors in Japan formed a special medical and agricultural research institute, and they have annual meetings to report their findings. Finally, on January 15th, 1966, this type of water ionizer was approved as a health improvement medical device by the Health and Rehabilitation Ministry of the Japanese Government.

Japanese-made water ionizers were first introduced to Korea in the 70's, and today they are also approved as medical devices by the government of South Korea. Korean-made household unit water ionizers were introduced in the United States in 1985 and a toxicity test was conducted by an independent testing lab in LA on April 14, 1986. The test found no toxicity in the alkaline water generated by the water ionizer. This testing was done according to FDA specified methods (FR vol 143 No. 163.81-1 1978).

6.3.2) Functions of the Water Ionizer

City water and well water

City supplied tap water contains an ample supply of acid minerals and alkaline minerals. They use acids to kill living organisms in the water supply. Then the water is too acidic to be sent out through the pipes. If this water is too acidic, it will leach out lead from soldered pipe joints. Lead is a poisonous metal. So limestone (carbonate of calcium) is added to make it alkaline. In general, city supplied tap water contains more alkaline minerals than the water from a private well.

Minerals in the tap water

The common alkaline minerals found in tap water are calcium, magnesium, sodium and potassium. The acid minerals are chlorine, sulfur and phosphorus. They are the same minerals found in our foods. Water gets its minerals from the soil and so does food. Therefore, it is not surprising that the same inorganic minerals are found in water and food.

A water ionizer has two water chambers with positive and negative electrodes. The negative electrode attracts positive minerals, which are alkaline minerals, to its chamber, while the positive electrode attracts negative minerals, which are acid minerals, to its chamber. The water going into the water ionizer has both minerals mixed together, but by the time the ionization process is through, one chamber has nothing but alkaline minerals and the other chamber, only acid minerals.

Ionization

The two chambers are separated by a special membrane with very tiny holes, holes so small that water molecules (usually in structured clusters under an electric field) cannot go through, but large enough for the ionized inorganic minerals to go through.

The original units had two one gallon chambers and it took about 15 to 20 minutes to completely ionize the water. The newer units don't have two large water storage chambers, but they have two small compartments for the water to flow through. The ionization takes place while water is running through the ionizer. (The newer units come with a charcoal filter to remove pollutants before the ionization process occurs.)

In other words, you turn on the water and push the switch, and instantly you get a stream of alkaline water from the top, and another stream of acid water from the bottom. The ionizer does not add any chemicals or minerals to the water. It only splits the minerals already in the water to the alkaline side and the acid side. If the water has no minerals, an ionizer cannot make alkaline or acid water.

Increase of oxygen in alkaline water

As shown in chapter 2, alkaline water has excess oxygen, more than the 2 to 1 ratio of H_2O water. The ionizer does not grab oxygen molecules from the air and put them in the alkaline water. What happens is that as the positively charged alkaline minerals come across the membrane into the alkaline chamber, they kick out one hydrogen atom from a water molecule and it joins with hydroxyl ions (OH^-).

The hydrogen ions (H^+) that have been kicked out receive an electron from the negative electrode to be de-ionized and become a hydrogen molecule (H_2) and bubble out of the water. In the newer machine, the ionization takes place in such a short period of time that when you catch the alkaline water in a glass you can see the tiny hydrogen bubbles moving up. The alkaline water initially looks cloudy but it clears up within a few seconds.

In the acid chamber the reverse phenomena take place and the oxygen is kicked out as O_2 gas, and the remaining water is acid water which is oxygen deficient.

Water pH

The pH of the ionized water depends upon the mineral contents in the tap water. City supplied tap water on the average has a pH of 7.7 to 8.4 and after ionization, the pH value range for the alkaline water is 9.5 to 10.4, and for the acid water is 4.2 to 5.5. Well water on the average has a pH of 7.3 to 7.9 and after ionization, the pH value range for the alkaline water is 8.9 to 9.5, and for the acid water is 5.2 to 6.0.

I had the opportunity to test the tap water in a Colorado mountain hotel. The tap water had a pH of 8.4 and after the ionization, the pH for the alkaline water was 8.7 and that of the 'acid water' was 7.0. I was surprised! The acid side came out neutral. This means that true mountain spring water has no acid minerals.

The alkaline water made by the ionizer is similar to true mountain spring water, for it is acid free alkaline water. But the alkaline water made in urban areas from city supplied tap water has as much as 100 times more alkaline minerals. (10.4 - 8.4 = 2 and $10^2 = 100$)

Commonly asked questions

Q1: Is any water with high pH good?

The higher the pH the more OH⁻ ions in the water. However, it is dangerous to conclude that any water with a high pH is good. I can add potassium cyanide into water to raise the pH, but that water would obviously be fatal. High pH water, obtained from 'drinkable' water by filtering out pollutants and removing acid minerals and enhancing alkaline minerals that were in the original water, is good. Not just any high pH water.

Q2: Could any harm be done by drinking too much alkaline water with a pH as high as 10?

The answer is no. As I demonstrated earlier in chapter 2, it takes 32 glasses of this alkaline water to neutralize the acidic effect of a glass of well-known brand cola with a pH of 2.5. Alkaline water with a pH of 11.5 will neutralize this cola drink on a one to one basis.

Q3: Can the ionizer produce alkaline water without creating acid water?

No, unless the original water was acid free to begin with. In that case the pH of the alkaline water will be about 0.3 higher than the original water pH and the acid side water pH will be near 7, a neutral value.

Q4: Can I buy alkaline water in the store?

Not yet. High pH alkaline water must be bottled in glass bottles. Plastic bottles allow carbon dioxide in the atmosphere to pass through and it forms carbonic acid, H_2CO_3, thus lowering the water pH. Because the alkaline water is saturated with calcium ions, the carbonic acid can form calcium carbonate, $CaCO_3$, and precipitate to the bottom of the water bottle.

Although it does not look clear, there is no harm in drinking the water. There is no loss of any alkaline minerals. The carbonic acid is a volatile acid and your lungs can breath CO_2 out and the full benefit of the original alkaline water will remain. But it is difficult to sell this slightly creamy looking water. If you are making alkaline water at home, it is perfectly alright to put it in a plastic bottle and to store it in the refrigerator for a couple of days, without losing its alkalinity.

I do visualize alkaline water eventually being sold in a glass jug or bottle. It should be a 'must' drink at the gym or spa, and people with any diet program should want it. It would be more expensive than any regular mineral water in a plastic bottle. People with private well water may want to buy the bottled alkaline water with higher pH rather than the alkaline water that they can make at home with an ionizer.

6.3.3) Interesting Facts About Alkaline and Acid Water

Disinfection without boiling

The Japanese government tested the disinfection power of ionization by inserting colon bacilli (bacteria that invade the lining of the colon) into the water to be ionized and tested the live bacilli counts before and after.

Colon bacilli/cc

Original water	Alkaline water		Acid water	
	immediately after ionization	1 hour after ionization	immediately after ionization	1 hour after ionization
1400	120	0	0	0

Bacteria that live in neutral water may not live in highly alkaline or acid water.

Plants and acid water

As I mentioned earlier, plant cells discard oxygen as its waste product. Therefore, most house plants love acid water. Cut flowers last longer with acid water. However, if you want your flowers to open up fully in a short time (say before your guests arrive), give them alkaline water. It is almost like aging plants more rapidly by giving them alkaline water. You can age animals faster by giving them acid water to drink.

Sprayed on the leaves and stems of plants, acid water prevents harmful insects from appearing. Rain water is acid, and the plants love rain water better than tap water. The trouble with 'acid rain' these days is that the acid in 'acid rain' is caused by industrial organic acids. In the good old days, people used to catch rain water to do their washing. By the way, acid water is actually soft water while alkaline water is hard.

Human skin and acid water

As mentioned before, human skin is acidic, but alkaline soap takes away acid from the skin. To replenish lost acids, I rinse my whole body with half a gallon of acid water after my shower. If taking a bath leaves you with dry skin, add a couple of gallons of acid water to the tub. Rinsing your hair with acid water will give you the effect of a hair conditioner.

If you use acid water for washing your face, the water will keep your skin fresh and clean and will protect your face from acne and discoloration. So-called pH balanced cosmetics are made to be acidic to match with your skin pH. You hear those commercials that talk about "the more you do the dishes, the smoother your hands get". Well, they are not kidding. Those detergents are acidic.

Warm acid water applied for about 20 minutes is good for athletes' foot and hemorrhoids. Acid water can decrease insect bite pains and neutralize the poison, and it can be soothing for burns. If you add mint flavor into the acid water, it becomes mouth-wash, and if you add a drop of perfume into the acid water, it becomes toilet cologne. Acid water stops bleeding, and that is the reason why mouth-wash is acidic and so is after-shave lotion.

Alkaline water and cooking

Alkaline water is good for cooking and making tea or coffee. Mixing fruit juices from frozen concentrates, you should use alkaline water. It will soften the acidity. Any water used in cooking that will wind up in your body should be alkaline water. For example cooking rice with alkaline water will neutralize phosphorus with calcium before you eat the rice, cutting the amount of phosphoric acid the rice will develop later in your body.

Boiling alkaline water will lower its pH because the carbon dioxide in the air will be mixed in the water quickly under heat. However, boiling water cannot boil away alkaline minerals; therefore, all the minerals are still there, combined with carbonates. The benefits of neutralizing acids in your body will all be there after the volatile carbonic acid is reduced to water by breathing CO_2s out.

Whisky sold on the market has a pH value of 5.2, which is acidic. Mixed with alkaline water with a pH of 9.5, one part to one, the resultant pH is 9.1, which is alkaline. Alkaline 'whisky and water' tastes mild, and the Japanese claim that you never get hangovers from drinking alkaline drinks.

6.4) The Coming Age of Far Infrared Waves

6.4.1) Backgrounds[12,17]

During the last decade, a silent revolution has been taking place in Japan in the fields of healing, preservation, cooking, drying and heating. It is the use and application of safe and efficient Far Infrared (FIR) Wave technology, replacing the potentially harmful micro wave technology.

When the overhead FIR heaters are turned on, people in the room feel warmth instantly but the air temperature remains cool, saving energy. One can boil an egg in a FIR boiler without water and the boiled egg can remain bacteria free for 30 days in room temperature. One can bake bread in a FIR oven in such a uniform manner that the air bubble sizes are uniform throughout the bread.

These things are not from science fiction but are actual events happening in Japan today. Between 1977 and 1987, more than 150 significant Japanese patents were granted in the field of FIR technology.[12]

6.4.2) What Are Far Infrared Waves?

Wave length of FIR

Electromagnetic waves between visible light and the microwave are called infrared waves. The wave lengths of infrared waves range from 0.76 micron to 1000 microns. One micron is one millionth of a meter or one thousandth of a millimeter (mm). Far infrared wave lengths of our interest range from 5 to 15 microns. The wave lengths of visible light range from 0.4 micron to 0.7 micron. The microwaves used in cooking have the wave lengths of 3 mm, and the microwave radars use 30 mm waves.

The natural resonant frequencies of molecules of water and organic substances are within the FIR wave frequencies; therefore, water and organic substances absorb energy easily form this radiated FIR wave. Since it is their resonant frequency, they vibrate vigorously at that frequency and become the radiator of the frequency as well as the receiver.

FIR penetrates deeply

Furthermore, since the FIR wave deeply penetrates organic substances and water (2 to 3 inches), the warming effect is very uniform. If organic substances are heated by near infrared (NIR) waves (wave lengths of 0.76 to 5 microns), the surface gets hotter than the interior, and the interior gets heated by conduction means from the surface.

In the winter time, we feel comfortable with a sweater on when the room air temperature is 80°F. However, in the summer time, we feel comfortable with short sleeve shirts on with the same room air temperature of 80°F. The explanation is that although the air temperature is the same, the walls and ceiling radiate FIR waves in the summer time that warm our bodies even more.

Temperature and radiation frequencies

The surface of any substance radiates electromagnetic waves in the dark. The energy spectrum versus the wave length curve resembles a bell curve. The peak amount of energy radiation is proportional to the 5th power of the absolute temperature of the surface, and the value of the wave length at the peak of the bell curve is inversely related to the absolute temperature.

[At -273.15°C (or -459.67°F) all the molecular level vibrations stop. This temperature is called absolute zero temperature. The absolute temperature is measured from this absolute zero point and up and is expressed in degree Kelvin (⁰K). Any temperature in ⁰C can be converted into ⁰K by adding 273.15. Any temperature in ⁰F can be converted into ⁰K by adding 459.67 and multiplying the sum by 5/9.]

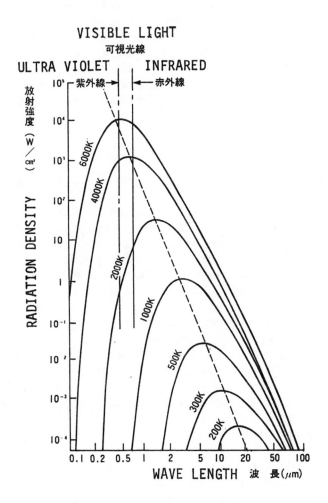

For example, at 300⁰K (80.33⁰F), the peak energy is 1.5 mW (milli-watt)/cm² at the wave length of 9.66 microns. At 500⁰K (440.33⁰F, hot oven temperature), the peak energy is 19.5 mW/cm² at the wave length of 5.8 microns. At 200⁰K (-99.67⁰F, deep freezing temperature), the peak energy is 0.2 mW/cm² at the wave length of 14.5 microns. The figure above is from "Up to Date

81

With Far Infrared Waves" by Yoshinobu Egawa.[12] It shows the variations of radiation density vs. wave length as a function of the temperature of black radiation surface.

Have you ever wondered how scientists can tell you the surface temperature of the sun? They measure the energy spectrum coming from the sun and determine the peak energy frequency and its wave length. From that information, they can figure out the surface temperature of the sun to be about 5500^0K (9440^0F). At that temperature, the peak surface energy radiated is about 3000 watts/cm^2 and the wave length is 0.48 micron which is the wave length of visible light, the boundary between green and blue.[13]

We live in a FIR temperature range

It is interesting to note that the temperature range of -100^0F to $+440^0F$ generates FIR waves with the peak frequency wave lengths ranging from 15 to 5 microns. From deep freeze to hot oven temperature, *we live in a FIR wave frequency range.* Our skin radiates 9.36 micron FIR wave since our body temperature is 97.7^0F. That is very close to the resonant frequency of a water molecule and it makes perfect sense since about 70% of our body is water. The army has FIR "binoculars" to spot the enemy at night.

A married couple sleeping together lives long. I am sure that there are some emotional benefits to help them, but another reason may be that while sleeping, they act as transmitters and receivers of FIR waves to each other. If you sleep alone, you act as a transmitter without receiving any FIR waves. People say that so-and-so has good vibrations. Well, when you are sitting together with someone and talking, you are sending away and receiving vibrations of FIR.

When an electronic wave of many different wave lengths is radiated on a substance, some waves are reflected away and some waves just pass through the substance. For instance, the visible light spectrum with very short wave lengths is reflected away while a radio frequency with a long wave length just passes through our body. However, some frequency wave bands are absorbed by the substance and the temperature of the substance rises. For our body and many other living organic substances, the FIR waves are the heat generating waves.

FIR wave is the safest energy source

We live in an environment of FIR waves and our body receives and radiates them. Among the energy spectrum coming from the sun, the FIR waves are the safest and the most beneficial electromagnetic energy sources available.

6.4.3) How to Generate Far Infrared Waves

There are three methods of generating FIR waves. The first method is to coat a metallic or ceramic surface with special ceramic material that is mixed with mineral oxides such as silica (SiO_2), alumina (Al_2O_3), etc. Depending upon the mixtures of the compounds, the surface can generate different wave lengths. When these coated metallic or ceramic surfaces are heated by means of conventional electric or gas means, the surface generates FIR waves. The amount of Fir wave generation can be regulated by controlling the amount of heat applied to the surface.

The second method used is to pass an electric current through carbon. When an electric current flows through carbon, the carbon generates FIR waves. In practice, they impregnate cotton sheets with a special carbon compound and let the current flow from one side of the sheet to the other in a sheet current form. Here again the amount of FIR wave generation can be regulated by controlling the magnitude of electric current or the duration of conduction time by a thermal sensor. They convert AC into DC first so that the carbon sheet does not generate 60 cycle induced current for the user.

The third method is to use room temperature FIR wave generating materials mixed with fabrics, paper, plastics and ceramics. As mentioned before, all surfaces radiate FIR waves as a function of surface temperature. However, this special compound of alumina (Al_2CO_3), and silica (SiO_2) can convert any normal energy into FIR waves in a most efficient manner so that in room temperature, the materials containing these compounds will generate more FIR waves than ordinary materials. The discovery of these mineral oxides and their capability to generate FIR waves was made by NASA with our tax money, while the Japanese were the first ones to reduce this discovery to practical uses.

6.4.4) Applications of Far Infrared Waves[12,17]

A FIR sleeping pad

The FIR sleeping pad comes in two sizes, twin and queen. The core of the pad is the carbon impregnated cotton sheet with two conducting strips on two opposing edges: right and left. When the power is on, converted dc current flows from one edge to the other in a sheet current form. As the current flows through the carbon sheet, it generates far infrared waves. The carbon sheet is protected by high quality polyurethane and then it is encased in a quilted polyester cover.

Unlike an electric blanket, the pad does not get hot when it is turned on. However, if you lie down on it, it warms the inside of your body and the part of the pad making contact with your skin gets warm. When any part of the pad gets higher than the selected temperature, the sheet current is cut off by thermal sensors distributed throughout the pad. It comes with an external control box where the AC is converted to DC and you can also adjust the desired temperature of the pad.

FIR sauna

A conventional sauna heats the air in the chamber to a high temperature and the air in turn heats our body. Since a FIR wave is not blocked by oxygen or nitrogen molecules, it radiates directly onto our body and it penetrates a couple of inches into our body. We can feel quite warm and perspire profusely, but our skin is not hurt by hot air. The chamber temperature is only 42°C (108°F).

FIR plastic plate

In the refrigerator, fish cannot stay fresh for more than three days. Placed on this FIR plate, fish can stay fresh for *five to seven days*. A protein molecule is surrounded by three distinctive layers of water.[17] The first layer is about one molecule thick and it is electrically (ion) bonded with the protein molecule. This water is called Z layer water, and this water freezes at a temperature of -80°C (-112°F). This is an important point to note in the art of deep freezing.

Surrounding the Z layer water molecules is the Y layer water which is 2 to 3 molecules thick. This Y layer water freezes at -10°C (14°F). The last layer (X layer) water is free water, not influenced by protein molecules. It freezes at 0°C (32°F) as we know very well. When these three layers of water are tightly held and active, life enzymes become active, protecting the protein molecule from the invading bacteria.

When a 10 micron FIR wave is applied to the water surrounding the protein molecule, the water gets active by the resonance phenomenon, thus keeping the life enzymes active, maintaining the integrity of the protein molecule. Remember the 10 micron FIR wave is at the resonant frequency of a water molecule, keeping the Z layer and Y layer waters active even when the X layer water is frozen.

The conventional preservation means is to simply refrigerate at or below -5°C. In lower temperature, the activities of bacteria slow down; however, life enzymes slow down more than bacteria. For this reason, meat spoils in the refrigerator, although more slowly than when it is left outside.

Bio-Mate discs

A cookie-sized ceramic disk, coated with FIR material and placed in regular pots and pans, can change the concept of cooking by changing the cooking water into structured water. Vegetables stay crisp in boiled water much longer. Tofu stays soft in boiled water for a longer period of time if this bio-mate disk is placed in the boiling water. These ceramic disks radiate a higher energy level in boiling water than in room temperature.

It is reported that if you place a few of these discs in hot bath tub water that you can stand higher temperatures. Ordinarily the tub water is unbearable at 108°F, but with these bio-mate discs radiating FIR waves, you don't feel uncomfortably hot at even 113°F. This allows you to perspire faster.

FIR socks and gloves

Coated with FIR material, socks and gloves radiate FIR waves when feet and hands touch the material, keeping the feet and hands warm in cold climates.

FIR hair dryer

Conventional hair dryers use near infrared heating to make the air hot, blowing it directly on to the head skin. FIR hair dryers operate much cooler and faster, not hurting the skin on the head so as to damage the roots of the hair.

FIR vest

How about a warm FIR vest for the skier or anyone who has to work outdoors in the cold of winter? It has a rechargeable battery which requires 15 hrs. of charging for 8 hrs. of use.

FIR range oven

The FIR range oven cooks more uniformly, and it does not damage valuable vitamins and flavors. It is not harmful like a microwave can be. When foods are cooked in a conventional manner, part of the food gets hot and the rest of it gets heated by conduction from that hot spot. This can damage the food. When cooked uniformly and simultaneously, this problem does not occur.

FIR waterless egg boiler

Boiling eggs in water heats the egg surface to 100°C. Cooking eggs does not require that high a temperature. In lower temperature water it takes a little longer, but cooking is more uniform. When cooking in FIR waves without water, the egg gets cooked at a much lower temperature and more uniformly both inside and out, without damaging vitamins and enzymes. The eggs remain bacteria free for 30 days at room temperature.

FIR ceramic paper

The application is similar to the FIR plastic plate except that you can fold it to wrap food. Used under shoe pads, it warms your feet while removing odors.

6.4.5) Far Infrared Wave Clinical Treatments in Japan

Dr. Toshiko Yamazaki, MD, owns a clinic in Japan where she continues her medical research. In her book "The Science of Far Infrared Wave Therapies"[30], she discusses the scientific principles of FIR treatment and she lists many interesting clinical case histories. Since the book is in Japanese, I am going to translate a couple of interesting cases for your information.

Treatment for cancer

"Mr. "I" is 63 years old with cancer of the esophageal orifice. Ever since he was young, he enjoyed all sorts of gourmet food and alcohol. Furthermore, he was a heavy smoker. He lived the kind of life that would eventually lead him into this type of illness. On April 5th, 1979, he came to my clinic complaining about chest pains on both sides. He said that he had an X-ray examination on his stomach by a previous physician and was told that it was normal. However, from listening to his symptoms, I doubted the so-called "normal" diagnosis. Upon examining him in our clinic, we noticed slight abnormalities and disorders in his neck and spinal bones around the waist. At the same time, from a blood test, we detected cirrhosis of the liver and chronic liver inflammation. We thought that it probably was the result of alcohol consumption.

Furthermore, the response to cancer was positive and based upon the test results of the "alpha-phosphate-protein", his liver condition seemed to be the result of problems occurring in other organs. We recommended a more detailed examination of his stomach, but we were refused. Then we sent him to a nearby radiology specialist for several X-ray shots of his spine. We explained the situation to the radiologist and requested him to some how take X-rays of his stomach. Taking pictures of his spine, neck, and waist, the doctor was successful in obtaining the X-ray pictures of his esophagus and stomach. The doctor called me immediately over the phone to inform me of the cancer of the esophageal orifice. Not only that, he told me that Mr. "I" would probably only have about one and a half months to live.

The doctor thought that Mr. "I" had left already, so he was rather frank and straight forward over the phone. Unfortunately, Mr. "I" was still in the waiting room waiting for his cab to arrive. So he heard everything! He came straight back to my office with the copies of the X-rays, completely depressed, and reported what he had heard.

I told him of a similar case where a patient with cancer of the esophagus was completely cured by tenaciously following the treatment procedure. And I was able to convince Mr. "I" to follow through with the treatment with us.

In those days, for his chest pain, Mr. "I" was taking aspirin family pain killers which were later taken off the market by the Ministry of Public Welfare because of their cancer causing side effects. Our conclusion was that Mr. "I" was suffering from the toxins produced by this aspirin family pain killer, and his cancer was caused directly by this medicine.

So the first steps were to excrete the poison that was the cause of the intoxication, to destroy the cancer cells, and to help him manage the pain. We employed a far infrared wave sauna to excrete the accumulated poison. The sauna method was selected for its ability to excrete poison and to suppress the growth of cancer cells through high temperature treatment by penetrating far infrared wave heat.

The treatment had tremendous effects on the chest pains. Perhaps because of the great amount of perspiration and the excretion of the accumulated harmful substances and the old wastes, he felt better every day. Since a high amount of perspiration also excretes valuable body minerals such as potassium, we paid special attention to his diet. The human body has to maintain a proper balance of potassium and sodium.

Mr. "I", who was diagnosed to live approximately one and a half months more, was discharged from the clinic after a 3 month stay.

Mr. "S" is a former wrestler. He weighed in over 220 pounds with a beautiful pot belly.

When he came to my clinic, he had a fist-sized bulge in the middle of his belly from stomach cancer. Moreover, since he was over 70 years old, he was told that they could not operate on him. He came to my clinic after he was told that he had only 3 more months to live.

Because of his obesity, we considered weight reduction. While watching a balanced diet, he underwent far infrared sauna treatment, losing about 45 pounds in two months. Furthermore, through the heat treatment effect of the far infrared sauna, the tumor got smaller in one month, and his stomach pains were reduced within a few days. Since his body strength was not down at this point, we gave him cancer suppressing pills and continued the daily heat therapy by far infrared waves. Originally stiff and hard belly walls gradually became soft and his appetite increased. With improved results, the cancer suppressing pills were stopped, fearing any side effects.

As a result of continued treatment in the clinic for one year, he was well enough to be discharged.

The fact that these kinds of serious patients could save their lives with virtually no symptoms can support the effectiveness of the heat treatment by far infrared waves."

Treatment of other diseases

Besides cancer, Dr. Yamazaki reports successful treatments of many other diseases by use of FIR waves, treatments not only by her but also by many other doctors. The list of diseases includes: stress induced chronic diarrhea; numbness; shoulder, back, and knee pain; rheumatism; low blood pressure; diabetes; radiation exposure related diseases; asthma; etc.

Dr. Yamazaki attributes the successes of the FIR wave treatments to the capability of FIR waves to remove toxins from the body. This may be an oversimplification, but in general, toxins in our body are acidic. Where the toxins are accumulated, blood circulation is blocked. Therefore FIR wave treatment is effective in expanding clogged up capillary vessels and successfully dissolving the hidden toxins into the blood and eventually out of the body via urine and perspiration.

I am not recommending people to buy FIR saunas or sleeping pads to cure their own diseases. What I am hoping is that more American doctors will experiment with new ideas, and treat their patients in the direction of helping their own body to heal their diseases, by strengthening their immune system or by removing acidic toxins. Too much emphasis is on the conventional treatment, which uses drugs to 'destroy' the unwanted elements at any cost. Usually the cost is our own immune system.

In the meantime, wise people can use these devices such as alkaline water makers, FIR saunas, FIR sleeping pads, etc., to prevent the accumulation of toxins and acidic wastes for the purpose of staying young and healthy forever.

Chapter 7

Other Non-Medicinal Health Improvement Devices

7.1) Japanese Government Approved Devices

According to a Japanese government publication[16], there are many government approved "health treatment" devices in Japan. In reference document 16, they list the names of the devices, the principles and the structures, and the affectivities and special notes in usages. The following translation of the publication is provided for your information. I do not claim the accuracy nor the validity of these statements.

"Low frequency treatment device

Applying two electrodes near the treatment area, a few milli-ampere current of 3 to 1200 hertz is allowed to flow through the affected area. It gives the effect of a massage and is effective in the recovery of fatigue, stiff shoulders, improving blood circulation, etc."

"Ultra short wave treatment device

Placing the affected area between two electric plates, apply several mega-hertz of voltage to the plates. The principle is that the body absorb the energy from this electromagnetic energy and converts it into heat to treat the affected area. It is a kind of heat treatment and is effective for improving blood circulation, neuralgia, muscle fatigue, stiff muscle, and improving the activities of the digestive system."

"Ultra sound treatment device

The device generates vibrations of 1000 kilohertz or there about. It uses the principle that any living organisms can absorb ultra sound energy and convert it into heat energy. Ultra sound can be used to destroy living organisms. For this reason, it is not approved as a household treatment device with the exception of the following two applications: eye treatment and bath tub application."

"Eye treatment ultra sound device

This device generates 12 kilohertz of vibration with the maximum power of 100 milli-watts per square centimeter. With limited output, it is safe. It is used to control irregularity in nearsightedness. Unless it is used under the specific guidance of a doctor, it is not as effective."

"Bath tub use ultra sound device

This is designed to apply the ultra sound energy of 45 kilohertz to the human body through hot tub water. It uses the power of cleaning and heating through the ultra sound frequency. It gives the effects of a whole body massage and cleansing. Anyone not allowed to take hot baths or massages should not use this device, and the direct application to ear and eye is prohibited."

"Myopia treatment device

There used to be a device sold by mail order which claimed to correct nearsightedness by flattening the eye crystal through pressuring the eyeballs. Such a device created dangers of causing astigmatism by undue pressure. With the exception of the ultrasonic eye care device, there is no other eye treatment device approved by the government."

"Vibrators

Sometimes called an electric massager, this device provides massage by converting electric energy into vibration energy. For the devices providing small vibrations, special attachments may be connected to massage your face, head, breasts, etc. These devices are used for massage in general and they help to relieve muscle tension, lessen fatigue, improve the blood circulations, relieve pain, etc."

"Suction vibrators

Applying a vacuum cleaner pipe directly to the skin pulls up only that part of the skin. Using this principle, the device pulls on and off very quickly, providing a suction type massage. The usage and effects are the same as the vibrators above."

"Electric potential treatment device

If 600 to 1000 volts of negative potential is applied to an insulated body, more calcium and sodium minerals in the circulating blood get ionized, thus changing an acidified body into an alkaline body. Although it uses a high voltage, since there is no current flowing, there is no danger. This device is sometimes called a static electric treatment device or high potential treatment device. It is effective for stiff shoulders, headaches, insomnia, and chronic constipation. It works for allergy patients; however, it is advised to consult a physician before using."

"Infrared treatment device

Infrared heat is not conduction heat but rather radiation heat; therefore, it can penetrate the skin. Since it has the characteristics of drying substances, it has been used for some time as a warming and/or drying treatment device. Recently they have been used as under the blanket warming devices. Unless it is used at an uncomfortably high temperature, it is safe to use for any extended time. Its main effect is deep heating. It is good for rejuvenation, improved blood circulation, relieving stiff and tired muscles, neuralgia, activating digestive organs, etc."

"Ultra violet treatment device

This device uses a low voltage mercury florescent light bulb to generate the ultra violet light. It is used to disinfect air in the kitchen and restaurants. It is effective against athlete's foot and under arm bacteria. If it is used with a special glass that blocks 2600 A^0 spectrum which is harmful to human eyes, it is good for artificial sun tanning use for the whole body. For that reason, it is good for the treatment of vitamin D deficiency. Large models are sold to be used in schools for the health of the students. Directly looking into the ultra violet light source should be avoided since that will harm the eyes."

"Acupressure balls

Several round ball like extrusions are placed 4 inches apart and you lie on your back to apply acupressure with your body weight. There are several different versions of this depending upon the distribution and the shapes of the extrusions. The effects and the applications are the same as a massage."

"Skin resistance measuring device

On the surface of the skin, there are spots where the conductivity is higher than the surrounding spot. These spots are known as the acupuncture or acupressure points. This device comes with two electrodes. Holding one electrode in one hand, you can move the other electrode along the skin surface to look for the highest current spot around the area. As you leave that spot, the current value will decrease. Using a 10 volt source, the current is very low. You can burn that spot or let the current flow through that spot for healing the reflex nerve system disorder. For healing with these spots, consult your physician."

"Magnetic treatment device

There are ions in the blood that are flowing. This could be considered to be a current flow. Applying a magnetic field to a current flow influences the flow. On the other hand, the blood is a conducting substance and a flow of conducting substance in a magnetic field generates electricity, also affecting the blood flow. Magnetic treatment devices contain permanent magnets with a surface magnetic strength of 500 to 800 gauss. Devices range from simple magnetic wrist bands, magnetic belts, magnetic seat cushions, magnetic sleeping pads, pillows, etc. It stimulates the flow of the blood close to where the magnets are located. The magnetic effect is the same whether it is a permanent or an electric magnet, as long as the current used is a direct current (DC)."

"Medical purpose water ionization device

Placing a solution of calcium compound in the positive polarity chamber, and regular water in the negative polarity chamber, divide the chamber with a porus ceramic, and then ionize the water. In the minus chamber alkaline water is formed and in the plus chamber acid water is formed. Drinking alkaline water cures chronic diarrhea, digestive problems, over acidity, etc. Acid water is used as an astringent solution for cosmetic uses."

The last item is the old water ionizer unit. In Japan, tap water doesn't contain many alkaline minerals; therefore, they had to put alkaline compounds into the acid chamber so that only the ionized calcium would move into the alkaline chamber. The state of the art water ionizer is much more convenient today.

They don't list far infrared devices, but they are considered to be covered under the infrared devices.

7.2) Magnetic System and Its Effect on the Human Body

Magnetic sleeping system

Magnetic devices have been available in this country for some time. They have a sleeping system with about 200 small permanent magnets distributed throughout the pad, downy and pillow. While you sleep you surround your body with magnetic flux. As described above, the blood contains many conducting substances such as iron in the hemoglobin. As these conducting substances move in the magnetic field, they generate electricity. This is the law of physics. We generate our house current using the same principle.

In the blood, generating electricity manifests itself as the ionization of blood. When any molecule is ionized, until it is mated with an equal and opposite charge, it is very active. In much the same way, a single person is very active in search for a mate while married couples are more stable. Since the magnetic field and your heart pumping energy force the separation of plus and minus ions, they are very active until they settle down with any opposite polarity molecule.

In the active state, each ion has an electric field which induces water to be hexagonally structured and active. Active ions in the blood have been detected to loosen and chip away plaque and cholesterol build-up in the arteries and it has been demonstrated that the use of a magnetic sleeping system lowers high blood pressure by slowly reducing the artery wall buildup of plaque.

Hard labor and over-working damage cells. Sleeping in the magnetic sleeping system helps to repair injured cells. If you had back aches and muscle cramps after a sudden laborious job, sleeping in the magnetic system will relieve the pain quickly.

Speaking of the repair of the body, a magnetic field helps bone growth. When you have a bone fracture, a magnetic field helps the bones to grow back, especially in the cases where the bone parts are not joined together.

Magnetic field prolongs mice life span

Dr. Okai of Kyorin University in Japan has discovered an increase of the life span of red blood cells in the bodies of mice under a strong magnetic field environment.[21] Dr. Okai also reports "The average life span of a mouse is approximately 308 days. On subjecting mice to a magnetic field of 4200 gauss, mice have been recorded to live to an average of 400 days." Dr. Okai reports that this may be due to the sterilizing action and other positive life prolonging attributes possessed by the magnetic field.

I have seen and experienced the effects of a magnetic sleeping system that helps to relieve aches and pains. When I mow my lawn and do the yard work for about 4 or 5 hours, I do feel aches and pains when I go to bed. It used to be that the following morning it was worse. I used to find some muscle pain in the morning in a place that I didn't feel pain the night before. However, if I sleep in the magnetic sleeping system, I feel much better in the morning.

Although I feel the effects and I recommend this magnetic sleeping system to people with back injury or people who stand all day long for their work, etc., I don't classify this system as a reverse aging device. The reason is that pulling out old waste products for the purpose of discarding them is not its main function.

Chapter 8

Natural Environment and Health

8.1) Planet Earth

We live on a very fragile planet. Just as our body requires balancing things in order to stay alive, the Earth must also balance things to survive. Some time ago I observed a completely sealed round glass bowl approximately 7 inches in diameter. The bowl was about 3/4 filled with water, and in it there were two tiny shrimp and a couple of water plants.

The waste products excreted by the shrimp were the food for the plants and the waste products from the plants were the food for the shrimp. The plants needed light from outside of the bowl in order to carry on photosynthesis to break up carbon dioxide into carbon and oxygen. Other than that the entire bowl was self sufficient and stayed alive for *two and a half years*, as of the time of my observation of it.

In many ways that reminded me of the delicate balance that we must maintain in order to keep this planet going. There is no question that the carbon dioxide content in the air is gradually increasing and that air and water pollution are slowly killing us. If there were five shrimp in that bowl the plants would not be able to supply enough oxygen for them and there would be too much carbon dioxide left in the bowl.

If scientists can figure out how to make carbohydrates from the air, this will reduce the carbon dioxide in the air. Until such time we have to learn to produce less carbon dioxide and give the plants a chance to catch up and produce more oxygen. Since many people are aware of these pollution problems and are trying their best to solve them, I am not going to address these pollution issues here.

What I would like to address here is a few of the less known natural environmental facts that the Creator has provided for the health and survival of mankind and life in general.

8.2) Nature's Two Kinds of Water

In the early days when I was just starting to drink alkaline water, I had to go to the Colorado mountains for business. Since it was a two week trip, I decided to take the ionizer and make alkaline water in the hotel room. Since I had the machine, I wanted to use the acid water to rinse my whole body after showering. That's when I realized that mountain spring water from the rocks contained no acid minerals. The pH of the water in the acid side chamber would not go below 7 no matter how long I had the machine on.

On the other hand, hot spring water is nothing but acid. You cannot smell phosphorus but you can definitely smell sulfur, the rotten egg odor near any hot springs. We know that people like to bathe in hot springs to get healthier skin. As I mentioned earlier, human skin is acidic in order to kill bacteria and viruses. Taking a bath in a hot spring is not just to restore skin acidity but also to melt out the old wastes into the blood so that they can be discharged from the body.

Nature provides two distinctively different waters: acid free alkaline water for drinking to wash out acid wastes within the body, and alkaline free acid water for bathing. Man-supplied city water has both kinds of minerals mixed together. I guess that it is easier to dump in chemicals than to extract them.

In the early days of man's history, we didn't eat so much acidic food nor drink so many acidic soft drinks; therefore, the amount of alkaline minerals in mountain spring water was sufficient. With our life style today, we need a higher concentration of alkaline minerals in the drinking water than what nature provides in mountain spring water.

The pH values of the ionized alkaline water made from mountain spring water are about 8.7 to 8.9. The pH values of the original mountain spring water before ionization are 8.4 to 8.6. Assuming that there are no acid minerals, each time you double the amount of alkaline minerals in the water the pH value increases by 0.3.

The pH values of typical city supplied water are also 8.4 to 8.6; however, the pH values of the alkaline water made from city water range from 9.3 to 10.5. This means that man made alkaline water has 10 to 100 times more alkaline minerals than natural mountain spring alkaline water. However, it takes 32 glasses of this 'strong' alkaline water to neutralize one glass of a man made acid drink: cola with the pH of 2.5!

8.3) Electric Ions in the Air

As there are plus minerals and minus minerals in the water, there are positive ions and negative ions in the air. Negative ions are molecules with extra electrons attached to them. Positive ions are molecules with some numbers of electrons missing. Atoms and molecules are electrically balanced and they are neutral in a stable state. It requires a certain level of electrical energy to lose an electron or to gain an electron. Some molecules are easily ionized while some others are hard to ionize. Under a strong electric field, they become easier to ionize.

When cosmic rays from the sun hit the air molecules, they break up molecules into positive and negative ions. Since the air is a good insulator, the ions swim around in the air. Electrically, the sky has positive potential with respect to the earth's ground potential; therefore, the positive ions will be attracted to the ground and the negative ions will be traveling upwards toward the clouds in the sky. Near the surface of the ground, there are more negative ions than positive ions, because the positive ions are dissipated by the negative ground nearby.

Nature's air cleaning system

Both positive ions and negative ions attach to pollutants or dust in the air, and they are either dragged down to the ground if the positive ions are attached to them or they are pulled up to the clouds if negative ions are attached to them. This is nature's way of cleansing the air.

In the highly polluted urban areas, cosmic rays cannot come down very low because of the thick layers of pollution. Therefore, there are not enough negative ions to clean the air. It is a vicious cycle. High in the mountains and near the ocean there is a high concentration of negative ions. The counts of negative ions are expressed in terms of the number of ions in a cubic centimeter (cc). Up in the mountains and near the ocean the negative ion counts are in the hundreds per cc, while in the city, the counts are generally in the single digits.

The winds blowing over the hot desert sands carry high counts of positive ions in the air. Also, there are more positive ions in the air before thunder storms. When two materials of different substance rub with each other, static electricity is generated. An electron (negative charge) sticks to one substance while an electron 'hole' (positive charge) sticks to the other substance. In this case the energy of friction is causing the separation of electrons from one molecule and attaching to another. This is why some synthetic material cloth clings to your body on a very dry day.

Effects of ions on health and mood

It is reported that positive ions create depressed moods while negative ions provide euphoria. There are several brands of household negative ion generators on the market for this very reason. They are trying to simulate mountain top atmospheric condition by shooting out high counts of negative ions into the room.

One thing that the users of the negative ion generators notice is that their room walls get dirty because the negative ions cling to the dirt and dust in the air and they are carried to the walls which are positive potential relative to the minus ions. One way to look at it is that the dirt goes to the walls instead of going into your lungs. Some later models shoot out negative ions for 10 seconds and then they change the generator body potential to a high plus voltage, collecting the ions with dirt particles back to the generator's dust collector.

There are a couple of theories as to why negative ions give euphoric feelings while positive ions create depression. The first theory is that negative ions can move about in the body very freely. Since a negative ion means an extra electron attached to a molecule, the movement of a negative ion means the movement of an electron, which is easy. Fast moving electrons give a molecular level massage and loosen up particles stuck in some places in the body.

Positive ions are molecules with one electron missing. They provide electric fields, but the movement of an electron "hole" is slow. In other words it provides tension, but the relief of tension by the movement of an ion (electron hole) is quite slow.

When ions travel through your body, they will travel through the path of highest conductivity. In chapter 7, we discussed high conduction point-finding devices. At that time it was brought out that these points correspond to the acupuncture points. So, when these ions travel through your body, they enter and leave your body through the acupuncture points, stimulating the body. Independent from your nerve network, there is an electric conduction network in your body.

If there were no high conduction network path, traveling electrons would disturb the nerve system. It is similar to a lightning rod on a building, protecting the building's plumbing and electrical wires from lightning. A traveling electron is stimulating substances along this conduction network. Acupuncture with needles also does the same thing.

The second theory is that negative ions increase alkalinity in the body while the positive ions increase acidity. As we know the water molecules are split into H^+ and OH^-. Negative ions will neutralize H^+ ions and the remaining OH^- ions will ionize normal un-ionized alkaline minerals. The net effect is to increase the alkalinity of the body. The reverse effects, i.e., the acidification of the body would be achieved with the positive ions.

These ions eventually leave the body. If they accumulate, you will get an electric shock when you touch a metallic object. The best such example is that when you are on a dry area walking on the carpet with rubber sole shoes on, you build up static electricity in your body. Then, if you touch a door knob, you get shocked. Ions and 'free radicals' cannot be stored in your body without changing your body's electric potential. Eventually they leave your body. But before they leave, they can change your body chemistry.

8.4) Electric Potential Gradient in the Air

With the surface of the earth as the reference voltage of zero volts, the upper atmosphere is tens of thousands of volts high. When a man stands on the ground at sea level, he experiences about 400 volts per meter of an electric potential gradient field. Since we are accustomed to this field and since there is no measurable amount of current flowing through our body, we do not feel the gradient field. But it is there, nevertheless.

Up on a mountain, say 100 meters high, the normal static potential would be 40,000 volts (400 x 100 = 40,000) if there were no real mountain there. The electric potential of an actual mountain is zero volts, the same as sea level, because the earth is a good conductor. The result is that up on a mountain, the potential gradient is much higher, as high as 1,500 volts per meter depending upon the shape of the terrain.

Potential gradient and lightning

The only time we feel the effects of this voltage gradient is when the gradient is so high that the air breaks down. Lightning is an example of this. It depends upon the humidity of the air, but when the gradient reaches 10,000 volts per centimeter, the air breaks down (gets ionized) and becomes a conductor. With high humidity it breaks down much more easily.

Ten thousand volts per centimeter seems high, but if two objects have a potential difference of only 10 volts and they are brought closer and closer to each other, before they touch each other the gap will reach as small as 1/1000th of a centimeter. At that instant the voltage gradient is 10,000 volts/cm, and the 'zap' will take place. I am sure that you all have had the experience of 'zap' when you touched a door knob in a dry area.

Interaction with the ions

Getting back to nature's voltage gradient, a man walking around or standing out in an open field is moving about in a voltage gradient field. As mentioned above, there are negative ions floating around in the atmosphere generally travelling upwards. This kind of condition lets the negative ions travel through his body from feet to head via a high conductivity path.

The higher the potential gradient and the more the negative ions in the atmosphere, the more ions that will travel through the human body, stimulating circulation and giving molecular level massages. This could be one more reason that people in the mountains live longer. Remember that they also have acid free alkaline water from the mountain springs.

Urban dwellings are destroying these natural benefits. We live and work in high rise structures which make the voltage gradient inside the structures to be zero by steel beams and conducting pipes and conduits and ducts. There are practically no naturally generated negative ions in these structures either. Not only that, the static electricity generated by polyester and other synthetic material are all positive ions. No wonder city dwellers are more depressed and more acidic than country dwellers.

8.5) Nature's Magnetic Field.

As we know, the earth has a magnetic field. Generally we call it the north pole and the south pole. What we mean by the north pole of a magnet is that the pole that points north. This means that the earth's magnet sitting at the "North Pole" of the earth is actually the south pole of a magnet.

An electric field line is radial, that is, it originates from a positive charge and terminates at a negative charge. It has a beginning and an end. A magnetic field line forms a loop and has no beginning or end. It goes around and around without anything physically flowing.

Electric current and magnetic field

Like a fast moving object creating air turbulence around that object, a fast moving electron creates a magnetic field spinning around the object perpendicular to the movement. If an electron is moving into a page of this book, the turbulence of the magnetic field created by this electron flow is circular in shape and flat on the page, spinning counterclockwise.

Since the definition of an electric current flow is the opposite direction of an electron flow, the current entering into a page of this book will create a magnetic field circulating on the page in a clockwise direction. If a current circulates on the face of a page in a counterclockwise forming a circular loop, the magnetic field lines will be circulating around the current path with the lines coming out from the page inside the current loop and going into the page outside the current loop. At the inside of the current loop, the front of the page will be called a north pole and the back of the page will be called a south pole.

Earth's magnetic field

Exactly how the earth's magnetic field is generated is not clear to scientists but from the behavior of the earth's magnetic field, they guess that the field is created by a flow of electrons approximately along the equator of the earth's core.[13] This flow apparently can go faster or slower, it can stop, and it can start in the opposite direction. The present direction of the field (from south to north) indicates that the present electron flow is counterclockwise as seen from the geographic north.

The current magnetic poles are not exactly on the geographic north and south poles; however, averaged over a period of 10,000 years, they coincide with that of the geographic poles. Scientists can figure the history of the earth's magnetic field, the location of the poles, and the polarities from the alignment of the iron particles in the sedimentary rock deposits, etc.

The most important facts about the earth's magnetic field on living things is that it can reverse itself. The earth's magnetic field reversed itself at irregular intervals that range from tens of thousands to millions of years. The last reversal occurred 730,000 years ago.[13] Reversals last 1000 years or more, during which time there is practically no magnetic field. This must adversely affect animals, some marine animals and some insects and birds, that rely on the earth's magnetic field for orientation.

Magnetic field deficiency syndrome

Orientation is not the only problem. Scientists are noting that the earth's magnetic field is weakening.[20] They calculate that during the past 500 years the earth's magnetic field strength has decreased a total of 50%. Currently it is decreasing at the rate of 0.05% per year. Dr. Nakagawa, director of Isuzu Hospital, Tokyo, Japan, in his thesis "Magnetic Field Deficiency Syndrome and Magnetic Treatment"[20] points out these facts and he lists syndromes of modern people that he relates to the magnetic field deficiency.

Dr. Nakagawa believes that the current trend of the decreasing strength of the earth's magnetic field is creating magnetic field deficiency syndrome. He states this: "I feel that there is a direct relationship between the decrease in the earth's magnetic field acting on the human body and the improvement of abnormal conditions of the human body by the application of magnetic fields."

Inside steel beam constructions, the magnetic field strength is further reduced. As copper provides a good conducting path for electric currents, magnetic substances such as iron, steel and nickel provide easy paths for magnetic field lines, thus leaving virtually no magnetic field for the surrounding space. Urban dwellings further reduce the earth's weak magnetic field.

Magnetic field and health

As mentioned earlier, any conducting substance moving in the presence of a magnetic field generates electricity. All our house currents are generated by this principle. Animals that navigate by means of the earth's magnetic field have memory devices that record the weak electricity generated by the earth's magnetic field and their own movements. What the doctors in Japan are discovering is the correlation between health improvements and the applications of permanent magnets to certain parts of the body.

From the current trend of diminishing earth's magnetic field strength, some scientists are warning that this may be the beginning of the earth's magnetic field reversal. Some scientists also find the correlations of the extinction of some species of animals with the reversal of the earth's magnetic field. Fortunately today's science can produce magnetic fields by means of a direct current.

8.6) Man Made Healthy Environment

Perhaps the first control of the environment by Homo sapiens was heating the room with fire. Since then we have learned many tricks that enable us to live comfortably in a hostile environment. We learned to humidify the air in a room, cooling the room by air-conditioning, eliminating dusts by mechanical filters and high potential dust collection means, etc.

Learning from nature, we can add some more improvements to Twenty-First Century homes. We can create mountain top-like electric fields in our room by placing a +2,000 volt electrical plate above the ceiling and the ground plate under the floor. There is no measurable current flow; therefore, not much power is consumed. Perhaps we can place a negative ion generator in each room also to simulate mountain top air.

In that case, I recommend some kind of easily removable and washable decorative material up on the ceiling under the +2,000 volt plate which will collect the dust in the room. The negative ions will attach themselves to the dust and bacteria in the air and will be travelling to the 2,000 volt plate. This will be a new way of cleaning the air in a room.

Another improvement may be to wrap the room with current conducting coils and pass low d.c. current to generate a magnetic field in the room to simulate the earth's magnetic field. This magnetic field should not be too strong because it will affect watches, computer discs, etc. With room-size coils you will not be able to generate strong magnetic fields in the room.

In the twenty-first century home, a water ionizer will be a 'must' appliance somehow built-in in the kitchen. Speaking of kitchens, microwave ovens will be replaced with the far infrared ovens. Waterbeds will be replaced with magnetic and far infrared sleeping systems. Home heating systems will utilize energy efficient far infrared heating methods.

All of these things will provide healthier, more comfortable and longer life. There will be a whole new industry for reverse aging. Looking back at the turn of the twentieth century, we have come a long way. Looking forward to the twenty-first century, so many exciting things are awaiting us. And what's so exciting is that many of you who are reading this book will be living long and healthy lives, and you will be able to actually see these things happen.

Chapter 9

Conventional Theories of Aging

Recently in this country, many articles have been written discussing the aging theory and potential solutions to slow down the effects of aging.[5,23] It is very interesting to note that almost every article refers to the future solution as the 'fountain of youth', yet nobody is looking for the solution in drinking water. I think that it is so obvious that everyone is missing it.

American researchers do not read many foreign research papers. They do not mention pH, acidity, alkalinity, or oxygen deficiency. In this chapter I am going to explain some of the conventional theories of aging and compare them with my theory.

Wear-and-tear theory

The wear-and-tear theory of aging states that metabolism produces toxic avengers that turn lipids in our cells rancid and proteins rusty. It further states that the damage accumulates until the organism falls apart like an old jalopy. This is partially correct. Metabolism does produce toxins and they turn cells rancid and proteins rusty if they are allowed to remain in the cells indefinitely.

The accumulated damage will eventually destroy cells. However, since the toxins are acidic, they can be neutralized and removed safely by alkaline substances, and damage to the cells need not take place. When we are young the body is more alkaline and therefore the wear-and-tear does not begin.

Planned obsolescence theory

The planned obsolescence theory of aging argues that aging is genetic, programmed into the organism like puberty. This theory may also be partially right. When a complex organism like the human body is being developed from a single cell, the development cannot take place all at once. There must be a planned order of development. However, once the mature body is fully developed, I believe that the timer in our body is the accumulation of acidic waste products which is synonymous with lower pH and lower oxygen.

One can speed up the timer by drinking highly acidic cola, or slow down or even reverse the timer by drinking high pH alkaline water. Another way to speed up the timer is to smoke. Smoking deprives our body of oxygen, lowering its pH. By the way, we can elevate our blood pressure by smoking.

Limited number of cell divisions

Another theory is the possibility of a limit in the number of cell divisions before the deterioration of a cell. Furthermore, they say that the cells from older people divided fewer times, and the cells from embryos divided the most.

Dr. Alexia Carrell[8] kept pieces of a chicken heart alive in a saline solution which contained minerals in the same proportion as chicken blood *for over 28 years!* The secret was that he changed this solution everyday. In other words, he disposed of the waste products daily. An ordinary chicken does not live anywhere near 28 years. This means that there is no limit in the number of cell divisions as long as the cell waste products are disposed of everyday.

The number of cell divisions may be limited as long as the waste products are not removed. I am sure that the cells from older people had more waste products in them to begin with and that is why they divided fewer times. Dr. Carrell's test makes us question the validity of the genetically programmed aging theory above also.

Glucose, the cause of aging

This theory suggests that one culprit of aging may be glucose (blood sugar), which makes proteins in and between our cells stick together, a reaction called cross-linking. What they don't say is the fact that sugar is a strong oxygen grabber. Sugar related products are used to strengthen plastic.

Each time plastic material goes through a heat cycle, it gets weak because oxygen in the atmosphere goes into the material under heat creating oxygen "holes". If sugar is mixed in the plastic material as it goes through the heat cycle, the sugar grabs the oxygen first, making the plastic stronger.

What I am saying is that if there was sufficient oxygen around the glucose, the glucose would be burnt completely becoming volatile carbonic acid, creating no cross-linking of proteins. All of us, young and old, eat carbohydrates, and the glucose is all around the cells no matter what our age may be. The problem is the lack of oxygen, not glucose.

Another way to look at it may be from the point of view of the three layers of water surrounding a protein molecule. When a cell loses alkalinity, the Y layer loses hexagonal structures and lets sugar or any other substance such as bacteria come in contact with the protein molecule. As Dr. Chun says, the activity of the Y layer water is critical in maintaining the integrity of protein and cell.[10] It is the acid build-up in the cell that allows the glucose to create cross-linking of proteins.

Cross-links, cause of many diseases

They attribute cross-links and glucose to many diseases such as diabetes, clouded eye lens, clogged arteries, kidney problems, lung damage, etc. All these things are the symptomatic results of too many acids and the lack of oxygen. They are looking at the symptoms rather than the basic causes. When you understand the simple basic cause, the solution is not too difficult to find. Too much candy and/or too many colas for a youngster can cause diabetes, because they hog oxygen away from the body.

They mention the immune system cells called macrophage which naturally recognize aging, cross-linked proteins and dispose of them. But they say that for *unknown* reasons the immune system cells become less efficient as we age. Based upon what Mr. Konno and Mr. Chun say about the water layers[17,10], I believe that when the Y layer water activities slow down or the hexagonal structures deteriorate as a result of acidification, the macrophage cells become inactive.

Whenever modern medicine says "for unknown reasons", I translate that to mean "because of acidification". Because the doctors are not paying attention to the acidity and the alkalinity of the waste products and the cells, to them the aging process becomes an "unknown reason".

Metabolic rate theory

They say that a lower metabolic rate slows down the aging process and that implies that we have a fixed amount of metabolism for a lifetime, and when we exceed that, we're gone. I agree with the first part of the statement but not with the last two parts. Remember the chicken heart experiment by Dr. Carrell?[8] There is no fixed amount of metabolism, etc. A slow metabolic rate means slow production of acidic wastes, and it means that the body has a better chance of getting rid of the wastes more completely.

If you are drinking alkaline water, you don't have to slow down the metabolic rate to dispose of the wastes more efficiently. I don't want to go hungry all the time just to live longer.

Free radical theory

I don't buy the theory that free radicals are the causes of aging, mainly because the aging process is an orderly progression rather than a random process by a stochastic mechanism. Negative ions in the atmosphere are free radicals and people up on the mountains live longer where there are more negative ions in the air. Free radicals may be another symptomatic result of an acidic condition and doctors are probably barking up the wrong tree again.

We are concerned with the carcinogenic effects of pollutants and radioactive fallouts. The major concern is the fact that they destroy healthy cells. Dead cells become acidic wastes which in turn can cause the destruction of other cells, unless they are disposed of safely and quickly. The fact that some people are affected more than others in the same environment can be explained by the fact that some people are more capable of disposing the wastes caused by pollutants and radio active fallout than others.

Yes, it is important to clean up our environment and eliminate the risk of radioactive fallout; however, in the mean time we can try to overcome the bad effects of these carcinogenic elements by helping our bodies to get rid of the wastes caused by these elements.

Genes theory

American gerontology tries to look for the answers in the genes. Improving human genes may help future generations but what about those of us who are already grown up and aging? They like to investigate complicated things but sometimes they overlook simple fundamental facts.

The simple fundamental fact is that no matter how much one can improve his or her genes, as long as the waste products are not cleansed from the cells, those cells will die.

Growth enzyme theory

Recently there was major media coverage of a "reverse aging" treatment by injecting growth enzymes, or hormones. They showed several people who got "younger" by this means. A few days later, word got around that the growth enzyme may actually allow benign tumors to begin to grow.

As cells get old, they do not split and grow as easily as young cells do. I attribute that to the acidification of the cells which makes the enzymes inactive. My approach is to increase the alkalinity in order to activate your own enzymes to grow. The injection of growth enzymes is the treatment of the symptoms rather than the cause. It is similar to the transplant of sheep embryo cells.

When you inject growth enzymes or sheep embryo cells, you have to be concerned about the side effects. However, when you reduce the acidity so that your own enzymes can become active, there is no fear about side effects. And as long as the acidic condition of the body remains, the new growth enzymes or the sheep embryo cells will eventually become inactive.

For this temporary rejuvenation, they were charging 30 to 60 thousand dollars.

Cryonics

Recently people are paying hundreds of thousand dollars to freeze their dead bodies or just the head, in hopes that someday Science may find: 1) a way to defrost them safely, 2) a means to revive them, 3) a cure for the cause of their death, and 4) a way to regenerate the whole body from just the defrosted head.

This really belongs to the category of "what will they think of next!" Chances are great that before scientists will find the first step, the company will go out of business. My advice to them would be to save their bone marrow cells until Science finds the way to develop a whole new person from a single cell.

They don't have to die first and it should be very inexpensive compared to cryopreservation. And I believe that the odds are better for Science to find this technology, because there is no need to revive a defrosted dead body.

If I am going to live 300 years by washing out my daily waste products, I am not so sure that I could stand another one of me, my clone, around.

None of the theories above give any simple solution. The proponents of each theory are hard at work trying to find pills to slow down the aging process. The more complicated the theory is, the more research money they can get to continue the work and therefore the job security.

Every researcher of anti-aging pills is saying that they are looking for the "fountain of youth", yet no one is investigating the drinking water. Worse, chances are that they are drinking some kind of soft drink.

Chapter 10

Conclusions and Postscript

10.1 Conclusions

Understanding the true cause of aging

The first step in reverse aging is to understand the cause and the process of aging. Then, one can stop the process by eliminating the cause. Today's medical science is busy working on the processes of aging without understanding their causes.

There are many different processes of aging depending upon the different parts of the body, but there is only one cause for all these different processes. It is the accumulation of acidic waste products within our body. Depending upon where the acids accumulate, the acids create different symptoms.

Modern medical science has missed it.

We live in an age of specialization, especially in the medical field. Doctors know so much about the narrow fields of their specialties that they cannot see the overall picture. That's why they are missing the simple cause, i.e., the accumulation of acidic wastes that our body produces as a natural part of our living process. The acidification process is very gradual and the process takes place throughout the body. That is why it is not in anyone's field of expertise.

For example, cancer research is divided in to many different fields: cancer of the breast, liver cancer, cancer of the kidneys, cancer of the pancreas, stomach cancer, lung cancer, etc. In the eyes of medical doctors, unless your specialty is the liver, you are not qualified to talk about liver cancer. No one will listen to you. The cause of acidification is not in the liver; therefore, liver specialists cannot find the cause of liver cancer. This is how we get lost in the maze of specialization.

Simple scientific approach

Fortunately, I am not a medical doctor; therefore, I am able to look at the aging process from a fresh point of view, independent from the conventional medical science approach. Since I am an engineer, a scientist and an inventor, my approach is chemical, physical and mathematical; that is, pure science rather than medical science. Medical science is more like statistical science; therefore, it requires large samples, preferably with a double blind method so that the psychology of a doctor or a patient will not influence the statistics.

The fact that alkaline neutralizes acid is elementary chemistry and it requires no statistical analysis or double blind test. The fact that there are 10×10^{20} more OH^- ions than H^+ ions in a 10 oz. glass of water with a pH of 10, and the fact that there are 316.2×10^{20} more H^+ ions than OH^- ions in a 10 oz. glass of cola with a pH of 2.5 are purely physical and mathematical, and again it requires no statistical analysis nor any double blind tests.

Based upon personal experience, I know that vitamins are good for your health, but I cannot explain the reason why they help in terms of pure science. The only way to prove that certain vitamins help certain parts of the body to function is a statistical analysis of a large sample of people, preferably using the double blind method over a long period of time to assure that there are no side effects. I have tried my best to stay away from those products that seemingly worked but that I could not explain with my scientific background.

Beginning of scientific research

It all started because my blood pressure dropped by simply drinking alkaline water for six weeks. I wanted to know how the water could do that. I wanted to make sure that it was not just a placebo effect. For me it was simple to know what I was drinking and how the ionizer made alkaline water. It was a case of simple physics and chemistry. What took me a while to study and appreciate were the elements of the foods that we eat and the waste products created from those foods. This in conjunction with the alkaline water made perfect sense.

Water

For this reason I devoted chapter 2 for the mathematical calculations of water, pH, H^+, OH^- and excess oxygen to share all that I know about water. The continuing research on water and its structures by many scientists is fascinating as we try to understand the functions of water in a living organism.

However, the most important thing to remember in chapter 2 is the fact that acid water is oxygen-deficient while alkaline water is rich with oxygen. When the amount of excess oxygen in alkaline water balances out the deficient oxygen in acid water in equal numbers, the water gets neutral. That's why it takes 32 glasses of alkaline water (with a pH of 10) to neutralize one glass of cola (with a pH of 2.5).

The next thing to remember is that the pH number is an exponent number of 10; therefore, a small difference in pH can mean a big difference in the number of oxygen or OH⁻ ions. The difference of 1 in a pH value means ten times the difference in the number of OH⁻ ions, and blood with a pH value of 7.45 contains 64.9% more excess oxygen than blood with a pH value of 7.30.

Food

In chapter 3, I have covered the chemical elements of the foods that we eat and all the waste products that the body produces. I don't expect people to remember all the chemical formulas, but the important facts to remember are that the majority of the wastes that our body produces are acidic and that all the wastes that we accumulate in our body are acidic. They are organic as well as inorganic acids.

Human body

During my study of this subject of aging, I've developed a great respect for the marvelous engineering that went into the design of a human body by the Creator. How it is designed to compensate for all the abuses that we inflict on ourselves is beyond my comprehension. This is covered in chapter 4. It is not important to understand all the chemical equations that explain what the body does to balance and maintain the pH with all the waste products that we continuously pump out.

What's important to remember from chapter 4 is this: even with the great balancing act that our body performs, because of our life styles, we wind up storing a gradually growing amount of waste products throughout our body, slowly causing acidification. Another important thing to remember is that acid coagulates blood, thus causing poor blood circulation around the places where the acids are accumulated. This in turn causes some organs to act sluggish and we start to see the symptomatic signs of aging.

The causes of adult diseases

In chapter 5, I discussed many different degenerative adult diseases that are the result of acid accumulation. I tried my best to explain the causes of these diseases, not from a medical point of view but from a scientific point of view. These diseases are what the Japanese doctors reported to have treated and cured in Japan by means of alkaline water and/or the elimination of toxins and wastes.

This book is not intended to teach people how to cure the diseases themselves. One should consult physicians for that. What this book is promoting is to understand the true causes of all these adult diseases and to prevent these diseases before they become incurable or before the body suffers irreversible damage.

Alkaline water is not medicine.

Remember, alkaline water is not medicine; neither is food. But doctors do recommend certain kinds of food for specific kinds of diseases such as high blood pressure, and gout. They also tell you what kinds of food not to eat.

What I am telling the world is to drink alkaline water in order to wash out acidic wastes, the universal cause of many adult diseases. I am also telling the world to stay away from soft drinks, especially colas because they are acidic. I explain the reasons in simple scientific terms.

What I am really hoping is that physicians will try these scientific methods with their patients so that they can find out for themselves what stages of diseases are the points of incurability, and what kind of symptoms mean that the body suffers irreversible damage. Physicians are best qualified for these types of judgments. The trouble is that most of the physicians that I talk to are skeptical about the alkaline water but they want a free ionizer.

Reverse aging methods and devices

In chapter 6, I describe the methods and devices of health improvement and reverse aging. Americans do it the *hard* way, while the Japanese do it the *easy* way! The American methods are diet and exercise, while the Japanese use scientific devices, such as water ionizers, far infrared devices, and magnetic devices.

In this country, the business of peddling youth is booming. As the first wave of baby boomers will be reaching 50 in the next decade, the interest in staying young forever is mushrooming. The easy method devices I have described in Chapter 6 are only beginning to be introduced into this country. If American companies come off of the conventional methods of superficial wrinkle treatments or devices for a symptomatic relief, and work on the development of devices that eliminate the fundamental cause of aging, they will catch-up with the Japanese in no time.

Bright future

I see the future of soft drink companies coming up with high pH drinks and distributing glass-bottled alkaline water. I expect to see the day when health and life insurance companies will offer lower premiums for the people who own alkaline water makers and/or other health improvement devices. I also see a whole new industry of far infrared wave applications and magnetic devices. The concept of air-conditioning a room for the healthiest environment will also open up new aspects for the building industry. Any company interested in futuristic product development should be looking into these fields.

The next frontier of Science should be the synthesis of food from air where four basic elements of food (carbon, nitrogen, hydrogen and oxygen) are plentiful. This would remove carbon dioxide from the air and solve the problem of green house effect. If the process could be carried out in water, inorganic minerals in the water could be combined in the synthetic food.

We live in a most exciting time. The cold war is coming to an end and the Middle East problem has united the rest of the civilized world. Although we still have to drive on freeways and interstate highways, we are no longer living under the threat of a nuclear holocaust. People are interested in good health and longevity. Fortunately for us, now there are sound scientific solutions. They do not require any special effort like diets and exercises do. All one needs is an open mind and the courage to take action.

10.2) Postscript

Are you a doctor?

Sometime ago I had to meet someone arriving at Miami International Airport. After parking my car I was walking toward the main terminal building, crossing a busy drive way over the designated pedestrian walkway. I was dragging along an empty luggage cart. When I almost reached the terminal, a car drove up and a woman was about to park her car on the walkway.

I said to her: "Lady, You are blocking the walkway." She looked at me and asked me: "Do you work here?" I looked back at her and asked her: "What difference does that make?" She thought about this for a moment and moved her car away without another word.

People ask me: "Are you a doctor?" I tell them no but I ask them: "What difference does that make?" Intelligent people make judgments by evaluating the information given to them. It's the non-intelligent people who ask if I am a medical doctor or not, because they cannot make a decision themselves, based upon simple facts. But they will accept a doctor's word even if the doctor didn't know anything about the subject.

I have written this book as simply as possible. There are some chemical equations, but they are there just to assure you that they are scientifically sound, not expecting you to know them. It's not important.

Important facts to remember

The important thing to know is that we age because we accumulate acidic waste products. Therefore, if we get rid of these wastes, especially the old ones, we can reverse the aging process. We can even eliminate the symptoms of adult diseases by these processes if no irreversible damage is done already.

The problem is that the aging process is slow and our body adapts to it, so that we do not notice the fact that we are getting old. As time goes by, we may notice the slowing down effects of lack of oxygen, but think that we feel great because there is NO PAIN. And we adjust to the slower life style, perfectly content, until such time when the deficiency of oxygen finally manifests itself into major catastrophic diseases. By the time one feels pain caused by the acid accumulation, the damage is severe. Often it is irreversible. One must start the process of reducing acidic wastes *before* the pain starts.

Diets and exercises do work to a certain extent, but there are scientific devices developed in Japan that can help you get rid of the accumulated acidic toxins more easily and effortlessly. Disabled people cannot exercise and very old people cannot exercise without some risks. These devices work no matter how busy you are, how old you are or how lazy you may be. As with diets and exercises, the results are not overnight; however, the process is the fastest among the methods using the natural process.

Better than life or health insurance

Ordinary insurance does not prolong your life, nor does it eliminate health problems...it pays when you die or when you are in a hospital, usually too late for anyone to do any good. And it stops paying when the sky rocketing hospital expenses run over the coverage limit.

Knowledge and action

At the beginning of this chapter, I said that the first step in reverse aging is to understand the cause and the process of aging. However, knowing the fact that alkaline water will help you dispose of acidic wastes does not help you at all unless you drink alkaline water yourself.

Too many people that I know are intellectually smart but they don't know how to translate their knowledge into action. To them the effect is just the same as if they didn't know.

We are our own nemeses.

In a free society, we control our own destiny. After all is said and done, it's your own decision if you are going to live a long, healthy life or not. The amounts of money people spend for automobiles, entertainment devices, etc. are so high that the excuse that "it costs too much" doesn't hold water. It's our closed minds that are our own nemeses.

My brother, Dr. Benjamin Whang, works in the U.S. government designing nuclear submarines. One summer he spent several months in the Pacific Islands with a group of neurosurgeons. When he came back, he told me a story that he heard from a surgeon.

During the French revolution, thousands of people were sentenced to be beheaded. A group of neurosurgeons conducted a massive experiment with the victims. The experiment was to try to communicate with a head after it was severed from its body. The families of the victims were compensated for their voluntary cooperation with the experiment.

The forms of the questions had to be answerable by a yes or a no. For yes, the eyes would blink once and for no, twice. (I would put one more condition in it that if the answer were may be, the eyes would wink.) I understand that the entire report is in the archives of the neurosurgeons' history. I don't remember all the details of the story as told to me by my brother, but there were several amazing details that stuck with me that I will never forget for as long as I live.

The surgeons spent many hours with the volunteers and their families to generate a list of questions. They wanted to make sure that they would not run out of questions. The surgeons were with the volunteer victims up to the last minute of execution, and everyone of the victims were asked the identical questions right before their head was cut off.

This last question was: "Do you think that you can answer the questions after your head is cut off?" There were several different answers. They were: "Yes.", "I don't know but I will try.", "Why not?", etc. to "I don't think I can." All those who said that they couldn't answer, could not answer even one question.

The first question that was asked of everyone right after their head was cut off was: "Do you feel pain?" All those who responded answered "no". The longest anyone could carry on a conversation was 3 and a half minutes. They didn't know if that meant that the head couldn't hear or that it couldn't blink its eyes. When some emotional questions were asked, the eyes even flowed tears. The neurosurgeons are sure that emotions are not in your heart but in your brain.

The point of this story is that if your mind is closed, you cannot do anything. You miss out on a lot in life; you are your own nemeses. Among the people who are reading this book, some will actually "reverse" their age and live long, healthy lives, and some will do nothing and unnecessarily continue the deterioration process of their bodies. It's up to you.

History repeats itself

When a concept or an institution begins, it starts out in simplicity, with a clear direction. As time goes by, the followers of the concept or the size of the institution grows larger and things inevitably become more complicated and confused. Sometimes it gets so complicated that it loses its original purpose and direction. Then someone comes up with a better and simpler concept. When this happens the typical response of the establishment is to discredit the new concept or individual. Only history will judge the validity of this new concept.

The original covenant between God and the Jews consisted of the simple Ten Commandments. However, in the days of Jesus Christ, Jews had difficult, tedious and complicated rules and regulations required for salvation. Jesus made it very simple. He made it so simple that He was charged with blasphemy and eventually was crucified on the Cross. It was His resurrection that finally convinced many, including his own disciples, that He was indeed the Son of God.

Then the Church that was started by Jesus' disciples grew so large and became so complicated by the time of Martin Luther that it started to stray from the original concept of salvation by grace. It took Martin Luther and his colleagues to start the Protestant movement, which brought the Church back to the basics. It took several centuries for the Roman Catholic Church to recognize the validity of the Protestant churches.

Many government rulers have displayed similar traits. Originally they may have started with a burning patriotism, but as their power bases grew, their interests seem to have been diverted to other causes.

It took several decades for the AMA to accept vitamins and special diets as a means to improve health. But as the health food industry has grown, it has become big business. Now there are many diverse opinions, based upon the product lines that they represent. What is interesting to note is that the group of people who advocate alkaline forming foods for good health insist that distilled water or RO filtered water is better than alkaline water. It makes you wonder whether they know what they are talking about or if they are simply interested in the money making aspect of the health food business.

Today's specializations in medicine and complications in diets make it virtually impossible for a layman to understand what's going on in health. My theory of aging and reverse aging makes it very simple to get healthy and to live a longer life. So simple, I am sure, that most of the orthodox medical doctors and dieticians will try to discredit me by asking me: "Are you a doctor?" or "Have you done any double blind tests?" My answer to the first question would be: "What difference does that make?" For the next question, it would be: "Pure science such as alkaline neutralizing acid does not require any double blind tests."

As I suggested earlier, anybody in doubt should ask an independent testing lab to conduct longevity tests on three groups of mice, grouped with similar ages and health conditions. The test should be done with three different kinds of water, namely: alkaline water, distilled water, and acid water or cola, while maintaining all other conditions equally. You can guess which group will live the longest and which will have the shortest lives. Sooner or later, time will convince the whole world.

Bibliography

1. Aihara, Herman - "Acid & Alkaline", George Ohsawa Macrobiotic Foundation, Oroville, CA, 1986

2. American Medical Association, The - "Family Medical Guide", Random House, New York, 1982

3. Backster, Cleve - "Evidence of a Primary Perception in Plant Life", International Journal of Parapsychology, Volume X, Number 4, Winter, 1968

4. Becker, Robert et el - "Body Electric", William Morrow, New York, 1985

5. Begley, Sharon, et el - "The Search For The Fountain of Youth", Newsweek, New York, March 5, 1990

6. Bolton, Brett - "Edgar Cayce Speaks", Avon Books, New York, 1969

7. Carque, Otto - "Vital Facts About Foods", Natural Brands, Los Angeles, 1933

8. Carrell, Alexia - "Man, The Unknown", Harper, New York, 1935

9. Choi, Kyu Wan, - "Ionized Water & Digestive Diseases", Korea Applied Science Research Center For Water, Seoul, Korea, 1989

10. Chun, Moo Shik - "Water and Health", Korea Applied Science Research Center For Water, Seoul, Korea, 1989

11. Davis, Adelle - "Let's Get Well", Harcourt, Brace & World, New York, 1965

12. Egawa, Yoshinobu - "Up to Date With Far Infrared Wave", Man and History Co., Tokyo, Japan, 1988

13. Emiliani, Cesare - "The Scientific Companion", John Wiley & Sons, Inc., 1988

14. Guyton, Arthur, M.D. - "Textbook of Medical Physiology", W.B. Saunders Co., Philadelphia, 1956

15. Hendler, Sheldon Saul, M.D. - "The Oxygen Breakthrough - 30 Days to an Illness-Free Life", William Morrow & Co., New York, NY, 1989

16. Japan Government Publication - "Table of Health Treatment Devices, Category Classification and Affectivity", Division of Drug Administration, Health & Rehabilitation Department, Tokyo Japan. Original Publication, Oct., 1965. Latest Edition, March, 1985

17. Konno, Kazuyoshi - "The Age of Far Infrared Wave", Man and History Co., Tokyo, Japan, 1986

18. McCabe, Ed - "O_2xygen Therapies", Energy Publications, Morrisville, NY, 1988

19. McGraw, Walter - "Please Don't Hurt the Daisies", Fate Magazine, Dec. 1969

20. Nakagawa, Kyoichi - "Magnetic Field Deficiency Syndrome and Magnetic Treatment", Japan Medical Journal, Tokyo, Japan, 1976

21. Okai, Hajime - "Earth Sciences", Kyorin University, Japan

22. Sano, Y. M. - "About the Ionized Water", Korea Applied Science Research Center For Water, Seoul, Korea, 1989

23. Simmons, John - "Is the Sand of Time Sugar?", Longevity, New York, June, 1990

24. Sung Bong - "History of Alkaline Water Maker", Seoul, Korea, 1985

25. Sung Bong - "Doctors Speak About Alkaline Water Clinical Treatment Cases", Seoul, Korea, 1985

26. Tompkins, Peter & Bird, Christopher - "The secret life of Plants", Harper & Row, New York, 1973

27. U.S. Government Printing Office, Washington D.C. - "The Yearbook of Agriculture, 1959

28. Warburg, Otto - "The Metabolism of Tumors", Constable and Co., London, England, 1930

29. Whang, Sang - "Amazing Facts about Health & Water", Sang Whang Enterprises, Inc., Miami, FL, 1988

30. Yamazaki, Toshiko - "Science of Far Infrared Wave Therapies", Man and History Co., Tokyo, Japan, 1987

AlkaLife®

AlkaLife® is a patented alkaline concentrate. It changes the ordinary drinking water into healthy alkaline water. Simply add two drops of it to an 8 to 10 oz. glass of drinking water.

The ratio of potassium and sodium in the human body is very important. **AlkaLife®** contains the correct ratio of potassium and sodium to provide alkalinity. Medical researches warn of too much sodium salt being bad for our health. A recent study published in the Lancet Medical Journal, as well as doctors at the Albert Einstein College of Medicine in New York, warn of the danger of no sodium salt intake. **AlkaLife®** contains a unique patented ratio of potassium to sodium that has been tested to be the most beneficial ratio for the average person. As a matter of fact, the ratio is almost the same as the potassium/sodium mineral content in the average human body.

There are many different alkaline additives on the market, make sure you ask for the original **AlkaLife®** by name, and do not accept any substitute.

AlkaLife® was invented by the author of <u>Reverse Aging</u>, after the book was published. A 1.2 oz. bottle, which lasts two months, is only $15.00 (shipping included).

To purchase, please contact

Sang Whang Enterprises, Inc.
8445 SW 148 Drive, Miami, FL 33158
1-888-261-0870
http//www.alkalife.com
E-mail: sang@alkalife.com